Contents

All-Ingredient Soup 5

Artisanal Veggie Broth 6

Countryside Dumplings And Stew 8

Beef Brisket And Mushroom Stew 11

Veggie Pot Pie........ 13

September's Best Soup 15

Central European Dinner 16

Parsnips And Turnips........ 19

Indian Turnips........ 20

North African Couscous 21

Chinese Potato Soup 23

Rustic Green Bean, Turnip, And Leeks Soup........ 24

Homemade Harissa(Classical North African Style) 26

Vegetarian Carrot Burgers 27

Peanut Honey Carrots 28

Lunch Box Almond And Cranberry Salad........ 29

Vegan Zucchin(Tunisian Style) 30

Spicy Garbanzo Dip........ 32

North African Breakfast........ 33

Classical Lentils........ 35

Harissa Crab Bake........ 36

Mashed Potato Alternative Of Parsnips With Carrots I........ 38

Mashed Potato Alternative Ii 40

Japanese Teriyaki Parsnips 41

Parsnip Burgers 42

Potato Chip Alternative With Parsnips 44

Rustic Oak Wood Soup 45

New England Style Chowder 48

November's Veggies 50

Hungry Bee Parsnips 51

Balsamic Parsnips And Brussels Sprouts 52

How To Cook Parsnips 53

Pennsylvania Freeway Parsnips 54

Frigid Winter Soup 56

Tuesday's Pancakes 57

Apple Dijon Veggie Roast 58

A Country Dinner 60

Mashed Potato Alternative 62

5-Ingredient Roots 63

Sweet Rutabagas Euroland 63

Country Wagon Stew 64

Easy Irish Dinner 66

Leek, Celery, And Tomato Soup 69

February Veggie Combo 71

Pot Roast Skillet 72

Parisian Veggie Bake 74
Cold Winter Chowder 76
Homemade Harissa(Classical Tunisian Style) 78
Rutabaga Stew 79
Honey Rutabaga Couscous 80
Russian Summertime Salad 82
Amish Inspired Relish 83
South American Salsa From Salvador 84
Pine Nut Pesto 85
Chicken With Seoul(Korean Chicken) 86
Orange Radish Relish 88
South Salinas Slaw 89
Korean Pickles 90
Milky Radishes 91
Fresh Veggie Platter 92
Alabama Slaw 93
Canadian Style Brown Sugar Carrots 94
A Stew In Dublin 95
Honey Butter Bae Carrots 97
North African Carrot Sesame Apricot Spread 98
4-Ingredient Carrots 99
Animal Crossing Carrot Cans 100
Hong Kong Carrot Vegetarian Dump Dinner 101

Garden Party Salad ... 102

Rising Sun Cakes ... 103

Radish Rejuvenation ... 105

Maria's Mexican Tacos ... 106

Filipino Style Tilapia ... 108

Radishes, Cucumber & Cabbage Spring Rolls ... 109

British Veggie Pastries ... 110

North Carolina Dinner ... 112

Skinny Vegetables Roast ... 114

ALL-INGREDIENT SOUP

Prep Time: 25 mins- **Total Time:** 8 hrs 25 mins

SERVINGS: 2

NUTRITIONALS VALUE

Calories 518 kcal, Fat 2.4 g, Carbohydrates 99.8g, Protein 29.9 g, Cholesterol 0 mg, Sodium 440 mg

INGREDIENTS

- 3 yellow potatoes (such as Klondike
- 1 tsp chili powder
- Goldust(R)), cubed
- 1/4 tsp ground cinnamon
- 1 (10 oz.) package frozen chopped spinach, 1/4 tsp dried basil thawed and drained
- 1/4 tsp paprika
- 2 large carrots, chopped
- 1/8 tsp ground turmeric
- 2 turnips, diced
- 1/8 tsp cayenne pepper
- 3 cloves garlic, minced
- 1/8 tsp ground ginger
- 3/4 C. dry lentils
- sea salt and ground black pepper to taste
- water, to cover
- Cindy's Magical Motorvatin' Spice Mix:

- 1/4 tsp chopped fresh basil

DIRECTIONS

Step 1

In a bowl, mix together the fresh basil, chili powder, cinnamon, dried basil, paprika, turmeric, cayenne pepper, ground ginger, sea salt and black pepper.

Step 2

In a slow cooker, mix together the vegetables and spice mixture.

Step 3

Add enough water to over the turnip mixture and gently, stir to combine.

Step 4

Set the slow cooker on High.

Step 5

Cook, covered for about 8 hours.

ARTISANAL VEGGIE BROTH

Prep Time: 20 mins- **Total Time:** 1 hr 40 mins

SERVINGS: 8

NUTRITIONALS VALUE

Calories 133 kcal, Fat 4 g, Carbohydrates 23.3g, Protein 3.5 g, Cholesterol 0 mg, Sodium 131 mg

INGREDIENTS

- 1 lb. celery
- 3 cloves garlic
- 1 1/2 lb. sweet onions
- 3 whole cloves

- 1 lb. carrots, cut into 1 inch pieces
- 1 bay leaf
- 1 lb. tomatoes, cored
- 6 whole black peppercorns
- 1 lb. green bell pepper, cut into 1 inch
- 1 bunch fresh parsley, chopped
- pieces
- 1 gallon water
- 1/2 lb. turnips, cubed
- 2 tbsp olive oil

DIRECTIONS

Step 1

Set your oven to 450 degrees F before doing anything else.

Step 2

Remove the leaves and tender inner parts of the celery and keep aside.

Step 3

In a large bowl, add the onions, carrots, tomatoes, bell peppers, turnips and olive oil and toss to coat.

Step 4

In a large roasting pan, place the vegetable mixture.

Step 5

Cook in the oven for about 1 hour, stirring after every 15 minutes.

Step 6

Transfer the browned vegetables into a large pan.

Step 7

Add the celery, garlic, cloves, bay leaf, pepper corns, Italian parsley and water and bring to a boil.

Step 8

Reduce the heat and simmer, uncovered till the liquid reduces to half.

Step 9

Through a colander, strain the broth into a large bowl.

COUNTRYSIDE DUMPLINGS AND STEW

Prep Time: 30 mins- **Total Time:** 3 hrs 40 mins

SERVINGS: 8

NUTRITIONALS VALUE

Calories 515 kcal, Fat 15.1 g, Carbohydrates 64.7g, Protein 29.7 g, Cholesterol 62 mg, Sodium 1261 mg

INGREDIENTS

- 1 tbsp extra-virgin olive oil
- 7 potatoes, peeled and quartered
- 1 onion, coarsely chopped
- 1 1/2 C. all-purpose flour
- 2 lb. cubed beef stew meat
- 2 tsp baking powder
- 2 tsp steak seasoning (such as Montreal
- 3/4 tsp salt

- Steak Seasoning(R)), divided
- 3 tbsp shortening
- 2 stalks celery, each cut into 4 pieces
- 3/4 C. milk
- 2 C. water
- 4 (.85 oz.) packages dry brown gravy mix
- 4 C. water
- 1 small turnip, peeled and quartered
- 4 carrots, peeled and quartered

DIRECTIONS

Step 1

In a large Dutch oven, heat the olive oil on medium-high heat.

Step 2

Stir in the onion, beef and 1 tsp of the steak seasoning.

Step 3

Add 1 more tsp of the steak seasoning, celery and cook for about 10 minutes.

Step 4

Add 2 C. of the water and bring to a boil, scraping the browned bits from the bottom of the pan.

Step 5

Reduce the heat and simmer, covered for about 2 hours.

Step 6

With a slotted spoon, transfer the beef into a bowl and keep aside.

Step 7

With a slotted spoon, remove the celery pieces and discard them.

Step 8

In a bowl, mix together the gravy mix and 4 C. of the water.

Step 9

Add the gravy mixture into the pan and bring to a boil.

Step 10

Add the beef, turnip and carrots and simmer, covered for about 20 minutes.

Step 11

Stir in the potatoes and simmer, covered for about 20 minutes.

Step 12

For the dumplings in a bowl, mix together the flour, baking powder and salt.

Step 13

With a pastry blender, cut the shortening into the flour mixture till a crumbly mixture forms.

Step 14

Add the milk, and gently mix till a dough forms.

Step 15

Transfer 2 C. of the gravy into a bowl and reserve.

Step 16

With heaping tbsp, place the dumplings in the pan and simmer, covered for about 20 minutes.

Step 17

Add the reserved gravy and gently, stir to combine.

Step 18

Serve hot.

BEEF BRISKET AND MUSHROOM STEW

Prep Time: 30 mins- **Total Time:** 3 hrs 30 mins

SERVINGS: 12

NUTRITIONALS VALUE

Calories 224 kcal, Fat 12.5 g, Carbohydrates 13g, Protein 11.1 g, Cholesterol 31 mg, Sodium 190 mg

INGREDIENTS

- 2 lb. beef brisket, trimmed and cut into
- 2 (12 fluid oz.) cans or bottles brown lager 2-inch pieces
- beer, optional
- salt and black pepper to taste
- 2 C. beef broth
- 2 tbsp all-purpose flour
- 1 C. diced potato
- 5 tbsp canola oil
- 1 tbsp malt vinegar
- 2 C. diced Portobello mushroom caps
- 4 sprigs fresh thyme, chopped
- 1 1/2 C. red pearl onions, peeled
- 2 sprigs fresh rosemary, chopped
- 1 C. diced carrot
- 1 C. diced celery root

- 1 C. diced turnip
- 2 cloves garlic, minced

DIRECTIONS

Step 1

In a bowl, add the brisket cubes, salt, pepper and flour and toss to coat well.

Step 2

In a Dutch oven, heat the canola oil on high heat and sear the brisket in small batches for about 5 minutes per batch.

Step 3

Transfer the brisket into a bowl and keep aside.

Step 4

In the same pan, add the Portobello mushrooms and cook for about 5 minutes.

Step 5

Transfer the mushrooms into a bowl and keep aside.

Step 6

In the same pan, add the pearl onions, carrot, celery root and turnips and cook for about 5 minutes.

Step 7

Add the garlic and cook for about 3 minutes.

Step 8

Transfer the vegetable mixture into a large bowl and keep aside.

Step 9

Return the beef to the pan with the beer and bring to a boil.

Step 10

Cook for about 8 minutes.

Step 11

Add the beef broth and bring to a boil.

Step 12

Reduce the heat to medium-low and simmer, covered for about 1 hour.

Step 13

Add the cooked vegetable mixture, potatoes and simmer, covered for about 1 hour.

Step 14

Stir in the cooked mushrooms, malt vinegar, thyme and rosemary and simmer a few minutes more.

Step 15

Season with the salt and pepper and serve.

VEGGIE POT PIE

Prep Time: 20 mins- **Total Time:** 1 hr

SERVINGS: 8

NUTRITIONALS VALUE

Calories 518 kcal, Fat 31.6 g, Carbohydrates 52.5g, Protein 7.4 g, Cholesterol 13 mg, Sodium 356 mg

INGREDIENTS

- 1 3/4 C. sweet potato, peeled and cut into
- 1 tbsp butter
- 2-inch chunks
- 1 C. chopped onion
- 1 3/4 C. red potatoes, peeled and cut into

- 2 tbsp butter
- 2-inch chunks
- 1 1/2 C. vegetable broth
- 1 3/4 C. parsnips, peeled and cut into
- 1/2 C. whole milk
- 2-inch chunks
- 3 tbsp all-purpose flour
- 1 3/4 C. carrots, peeled and cut into
- 1 1/2 tsp curry powder
- 2-inch chunks
- 1 (17.25 oz.) package frozen puff pastry,
- 2 tbsp olive oil
- thawed and cut into four 5-inch squares
- sea salt and ground black pepper to taste

DIRECTIONS

Step 1

Set your oven to 400 degrees F before doing anything else.

Step 2

In a large roasting pan, add the sweet potato, red potatoes, parsnips, carrots, olive oil, sea salt and black pepper and toss to coat well.

Step 3

Cook in the oven for about 20-30 minutes.

Step 4

In a pan, melt 1 tbsp of the butter on medium heat and sauté the onion for about 3-5 minutes.

Step 5

Add the sweet potato mixture, 2 tbsp of the butter, salt and black pepper and sauté for about 2-3 minutes.

Step 6

In another pan, add the vegetable broth and milk on medium heat and bring to a boil.

Step 7

Add the flour and curry powder and gently stir to combine.

Step 8

Slowly, add the broth mixture into the pan of the sweet potato mixture and cook for about 3 minutes, stirring occasionally.

Step 9

Divide the mixture into 4 pot pie dishes evenly and top each with a puff pastry square.

Step 10

Cook in the oven for about 17-20 minutes.

SEPTEMBER'S BEST SOUP

Prep Time: 20 mins- **Total Time:** 50 mins

SERVINGS: 4

NUTRITIONALS VALUE

Calories 204 kcal, Fat 13 g, Carbohydrates 22.3g, Protein 2.7 g, Cholesterol 24 mg, Sodium 854 mg

INGREDIENTS

- 3 tbsp butter
- 1 bay leaf
- 1 tbsp olive oil

- 1 tbsp honey
- 2 C. cubed butternut squash
- 1/4 tsp ground black pepper
- 2 C. cubed turnips
- 1/4 tsp ground nutmeg
- 1 C. thinly sliced celery
- 3/8 tsp ground coriander
- 1 onion, diced
- 1/8 tsp cayenne pepper
- 3 cloves garlic, minced
- salt to taste (optional)
- 1 quart chicken stock

DIRECTIONS

Step 1

In a skillet, melt the butter on medium heat and cook the butternut squash, turnips, celery, onion and garlic for about 10 minutes.

Step 2

Meanwhile in a large pan, add the chicken stock on medium heat and bring to a simmer.

Step 3

Add the vegetables, bay leaf, honey, pepper, nutmeg, coriander, cayenne pepper and salt and simmer for about 20 minutes.

Step 4

Discard the bay leaf while serving.

CENTRAL EUROPEAN DINNER

Prep Time: 30 mins- **Total Time:** 11 hrs 30 mins

SERVINGS: 6

NUTRITIONALS VALUE

Calories 958 kcal, Fat 23.7 g, Carbohydrates 143.9g, Protein 45.8 g, Cholesterol 108 mg, Sodium 1434 mg

INGREDIENTS

- 1 (3 lb.) boneless corned beef brisket
- Dumplings:
- 1 1/2 C. yellow split peas
- 1 1/2 C. all-purpose flour
- 1 large head cabbage, quartered
- 2 tsp white sugar
- 1 medium turnip, peeled and cubed
- 2 tsp baking powder
- 6 carrots, peeled and cut in chunks
- 3/4 C. water
- 6 large potatoes, peeled and quartered
- 2 tbsp butter
- 1/2 tsp black pepper

DIRECTIONS

Step 1

In a large bowl of cold water, soak the corned beef and refrigerate for overnight.

Step 2

In a triple layer of cheesecloth, tie the yellow peas tightly.

Step 3

Drain the beef and transfer into a large Dutch oven with the yellow pea's bag and enough fresh water to cover and bring to a boil.

Step 4

Reduce the heat and simmer for about 2 hours.

Step 5

Add the chopped cabbage, turnip and carrots and simmer for about 25 minutes.

Step 6

Add the chopped potatoes and simmer for about 20-25 minutes.

Step 7

Meanwhile for the dumpling dough in a bowl, mix together the flour, sugar, and baking powder. Slowly, add enough water and mix till a pastry dough forms.

Step 8

Divide the dough into 6 equal sized balls.

Step 9

During the last 5-10 minutes of the cooking of the vegetables, place the dough balls over the vegetables. Cook, covered for about 7 minutes.

Step 10

Transfer the vegetables mixture into a warm serving platter.

Step 11

Remove the peas from the cheesecloth bag and return into the pan.

Step 12

Add the butter and black pepper and mash well.

Step 13

Serve the mashed peas alongside the beef and vegetables.

PARSNIPS AND TURNIPS

Prep Time: 15 mins- **Total Time:** 40 mins

SERVINGS: 6

NUTRITIONALS VALUE

Calories 354 kcal, Fat 23.4 g, Carbohydrates 36.2g, Protein 3.3 g, Cholesterol 68 mg, Sodium 266 mg

INGREDIENTS

- 6 carrots, peeled and chopped
- 1 pinch cayenne pepper
- 4 large parsnips, peeled and chopped
- salt and ground black pepper to taste
- 2 turnips, peeled and chopped
- 1/2 C. butter
- 1/2 C. heavy whipping cream
- 1/4 tsp ground nutmeg

DIRECTIONS

Step 1

In a pan, add the carrots, parsnips, turnips and enough lightly salted water to cover and bring to a boil.

Step 2

Cook for about 25 minutes.

Step 3

Drain well and return the vegetables to the pan.

Step 4

Add the butter, cream, nutmeg, cayenne pepper, salt and black pepper and with a potato masher, mash roughly.

INDIAN TURNIPS

Prep Time: 5 mins- **Total Time:** 25 mins

SERVINGS: 4

NUTRITIONALS VALUE

Calories 149 kcal, Fat 14.1 g, Carbohydrates 5.7g, Protein 1 g, Cholesterol 0 mg, Sodium 359 mg

INGREDIENTS

- 3 turnips, diced
- 1 1/2 tsp ground red pepper
- 1/4 C. vegetable oil
- 1 tsp ground turmeric
- 1/2 tsp yellow mustard seed
- salt to taste
- 1/2 tsp black mustard seed

DIRECTIONS

Step 1

In a large pan, add the turnips and enough salted water to cover and bring to a boil on high heat.

Step 2

Reduce the heat to medium-low and simmer, covered for about 15-20 minutes.

Step 3

Drain and keep aside to steam dry for 1-2 minutes.

Step 4

In a large skillet, heat the oil on medium-high heat and sauté the yellow mustard seeds, black mustard seeds and turmeric till the mustard seeds starts to pop.

Step 5

Add the turnips and cook for about 5 minutes.

Step 6

Season with the salt and serve.

NORTH AFRICAN COUSCOUS

Prep Time: 45 mins- **Total Time:** 1 hr 30 mins

SERVINGS: 6

NUTRITIONALS VALUE

Calories 934 kcal, Fat 39 g, Carbohydrates 80.5g, Protein 62.2 g, Cholesterol 169 mg, Sodium 601 mg

INGREDIENTS

- 3 tbsp olive oil
- 2 C. chicken stock
- 2 lbs chicken thighs
- 2 tsps thyme
- 12 oz. Italian sausage, optional
- 1 tsp turmeric
- 1 tbsp diced garlic
- 1 tsp cayenne pepper
- 2 onions, minced
- 1/4 tsp harissa, see appendix
- 2 carrots, julienned

- 1 bay leaf
- 1/2 stalk celery, chunked
- 2 zucchini, cut in half
- 1 rutabaga, parsnip, or turnip, chunked
- 2 C. couscous
- 1/2 green bell pepper, julienned
- 2 C. chicken stock
- 1/2 red bell pepper, julienned
- 1/2 C. plain yogurt
- 1 can diced tomatoes
- 1 can garbanzo beans

DIRECTIONS

Step 1

Brown your chicken thighs all over in olive oil.

Step 2

Add in your sausage and cook everything until fully done. Once it has cooled dice the sausage into pieces.

Step 3

Now stir fry your garlic and onions until tender and see-through then combine in: stock, bay leaf, carrots, harissa, beans, celery, cayenne, tomatoes, turmeric, rutabaga, thyme, red and green peppers. Cook for 2 more mins before adding your chicken and sausage.

Step 4

Place a lid on the pan and cook for 35 mins until chicken is fully done.

Step 5

Add your zucchini and cook for 7 more mins.

Step 6

Meanwhile boil 2 C. of chicken stock then pour it over your couscous in a bowl along with 2 tbsps of olive oil. Place a covering on the bowl and let it sit for at least 10 mins.

Step 7

When plating the dish first layer couscous then some chicken mix and then some yogurt.

Step 8

Enjoy.

CHINESE POTATO SOUP

Prep Time: 10 mins- **Total Time:** 1 hr 55 mins

SERVINGS: 3

NUTRITIONALS VALUE

Calories 255 kcal, Fat 2.8 g, Carbohydrates 47.2g, Protein 11.6 g, Cholesterol 19 mg, Sodium 77 mg

INGREDIENTS

- 3 potatoes, cubed
- 5 cloves garlic, minced
- 1 carrot, diced
- 1 chicken leg
- 1 turnip, diced
- salt and pepper to taste
- 1 onion, diced

DIRECTIONS

Step 1

Get the following boiling: water, potatoes, chicken, carrots, garlic, turnips, and onions.

Step 2

Once the mix is boiling, set the heat to a low level.

Step 3

Cook the mix for 50 mins then add some pepper and salt.

Step 4

Take out the chicken legs and remove their meat, once the chicken is cool enough to handle.

Step 5

Place the meat back into the soup. Throw away the bones and skin.

Step 6

Continue cooking the soup for 35 more mins.

Step 7

Enjoy.

RUSTIC GREEN BEAN, TURNIP, AND LEEKS SOUP

Prep Time: 25 mins- **Total Time:** 1 hr 35 mins

SERVINGS: 12

NUTRITIONALS VALUE

Calories 146 kcal, Fat 5.6 g, Carbohydrates 16.6g, Protein 8.4 g, Cholesterol 10 mg, Sodium 1013 mg

INGREDIENTS

- 12 C. chicken broth
- 1/2 C. chopped green bell pepper
- 1 C. chopped fresh green beans

- 1 tsp salt
- 1 1/4 C. cubed turnips
- 1/2 tsp ground black pepper
- 1/2 C. chopped leeks
- 1/4 C. butter
- 1/2 C. chopped carrots
- 1/2 C. all-purpose flour
- 1/3 C. barley
- 1 1/2 lb. Brussels sprouts, trimmed and
- cut in half

DIRECTIONS

Step 1

In a large soup pan, add the chicken broth and bring to a boil on medium-high heat.

Step 2

Add the beans, turnips, leeks, carrots and barley and reduce the heat to medium.

Step 3

Simmer for about 30 minutes.

Step 4

Add the Brussels sprouts, green pepper, salt and pepper and simmer for about 30 minutes.

Step 5

In a small frying pan, melt the butter on medium heat and cook the flour, beating continuously till smooth.

Step 6

Stir the flour mixture into the soup and simmer for about 10 minutes.

HOMEMADE HARISSA(CLASSICAL NORTH AFRICAN STYLE)

Prep Time: 20 mins- **Total Time:** 20 mins

SERVINGS: 40

NUTRITIONALS VALUE

Calories 28 kcal, Fat 2.8 , Carbohydrates 0.9g, Protein 0.2 g, Cholesterol 0 m, Sodium 176 mg

INGREDIENTS

- 6 oz. bird's eye chilies, seeded and stems
- 1 tbsp dried mint
- removed
- 1/2 C. chopped fresh cilantro
- 12 cloves garlic, peeled
- 1/2 C. olive oil
- 1 tbsp coriander, ground
- 1 tbsp ground cumin
- 1 tbsp salt

DIRECTIONS

Step 1

Add the following to the bowl a food processor: chilies, cilantro, garlic, salt mint, coriander, and cumin.

Step 2

Pulse the mix until it is smooth then add in some olive oil and pulse the mix a few more times.

Step 3

Place the mix in jar and top everything with the rest of the oil.

Step 4

Enjoy.

VEGETARIAN CARROT BURGERS

Prep Time: 10 mins- **Total Time:** 1 hr

SERVINGS: 4

NUTRITIONALS VALUE

Calories 236 kcal, Fat 12.6 g, Carbohydrates 22.5g, Protein 9.1 g, Cholesterol 186 mg, Sodium 489 mg

INGREDIENTS

- 1 pound carrots, grated
- 1/2 teaspoon salt
- 1 clove garlic, minced
- 1 pinch ground black pepper
- 4 eggs
- 2 tablespoons vegetable oil
- 1/4 cup all-purpose flour
- 1/4 cup bread crumbs or matzo meal

DIRECTIONS

Step 1

Combine the following in a big bowl: black pepper, carrots, salt, garlic, bread crumbs, flour, and eggs.

Step 2

Get your oil hot in a skillet then shape the crumbly mix into burgers. Fry each burger until it is crispy on both sides.

Step 3

Enjoy.

PEANUT HONEY CARROTS

Prep Time: 10 mins- **Total Time:** 50 mins

SERVINGS: 4

NUTRITIONALS VALUE

Calories 204 kcal, Fat 10.4 g, Carbohydrates 29.1g, Protein 1.2 g, Cholesterol 0 mg, Sodium 85 mg

INGREDIENTS

- 8 carrots, peeled
- salt and ground black pepper to taste
- 3 tablespoons peanut oil
- 1/4 cup honey

DIRECTIONS

Step 1

Set your oven to 350 degrees before doing anything else.

Step 2

Get a casserole dish for your carrots and coat them evenly with the peanut oil. Toss everything then top the veggies with the honey and toss them again. Add your pepper and salt and toss one more time.

Step 3

Cook the carrots in the oven for 50 mins.

Step 4

Enjoy.

LUNCH BOX ALMOND AND CRANBERRY SALAD

Prep Time: 30 mins- **Total Time:** 1 hr 10 mins

SERVINGS: 6

NUTRITIONALS VALUE

Calories 295 kcal, Fat 19.7 g, Carbohydrates 23.8g, Protein 7.6 g, Cholesterol 14 mg, Sodium 370 mg

INGREDIENTS

- 2 pounds carrots, peeled and thinly
- 1 tablespoon cider vinegar
- sliced on the diagonal
- 1/3 cup dried cranberries
- 1/2 cup slivered almonds
- 1 (4 ounce) package crumbled Danish
- 2 cloves garlic, minced
- blue cheese
- 1/4 cup extra-virgin olive oil
- 2 cups arugula
- salt and ground black pepper to taste
- 1 teaspoon honey

DIRECTIONS

Step 1

Set your oven to 400 degrees before doing anything else.

Step 2

Get a bowl, combine: garlic, carrots, and almonds. Top everything with the olive oil then with pepper and salt.

Step 3

Lay the carrots into a casserole dish. Then cook them in the oven for 35 mins. Let the carrots lose their heat then place them in a bowl. Top the carrots with your vinegar and honey and combine everything nicely.

Step 4

Combine in the blue cheese and cranberries and combine the salad again. Add in the arugula and divide the salad into servings or place the mix in the fridge covered until you are ready to eat.

Step 5

Enjoy.

VEGAN ZUCCHIN(TUNISIAN STYLE)

Prep Time: 15 mins- **Total Time:** 25 mins

SERVINGS: 3

NUTRITIONALS VALUE

Calories 111.8, Cholesterol 0.0mg, Sodium 34.8mg, Carbohydrates 6.7g, Protein 1.4g

INGREDIENTS

- 1/2 lb zucchini
- juice of half lemon
- 2 carrots

- plain yogurt
- 2 tbsps olive oil
- fresh cilantro
- 1 garlic clove, diced
- salt, to taste
- 1/2 tbsp harissa, see appendix
- black pepper, to taste
- 1/4 tsp ground cumin
- 1/4 tsp caraway seed

DIRECTIONS

Step 1

Get a bowl, combine: olive oil, garlic clove, harissa, cumin, caraway, and lemon juice.

Step 2

Get a casserole dish and place your carrots and zucchini in it. Top them with the olive oil mix evenly then place a covering of plastic on the dish and let the veggie sit for 60 mins.

Step 3

Now get a grill hot and coat the grate with oil.

Step 4

Grill the veggies for about 10 mins or until you find that the outside is slightly charred but the inside is tender.

Step 5

Place the veggies in a dish for serving then top them with some pepper and salt.

Step 6

Now add your cilantro evenly over everything and serve the dish with some yogurt.

Step 7

Enjoy.

SPICY GARBANZO DIP

Prep Time: 30 mins- **Total Time:** 9 hrs

SERVINGS: 1

NUTRITIONALS VALUE

Calories 840.8, Cholesterol 0.0mg, Sodium 58.1mg, Carbohydrates 108.1g, Protein 30.3g

INGREDIENTS

- 2 C. dried garbanzo beans
- 2 tbsps olive oil
- 1 carrot, peeled and cut in half
- 1 tsp harissa, see appendix
- 1 medium Spanish onion, cut in half
- 1 tsp ground cumin
- 4 garlic cloves, peeled
- 2 eggplants, cut in half lengthwise
- 1/4 C. olive oil
- 2 birds eye chilies, cut in half, seeds
- removed

DIRECTIONS

Step 1

Let your chickpeas sit submerged in water overnight. Then remove all the liquids. Get the following boiling in water, in a large pot: 4 C. of water, chickpeas, onions, and carrots. Once the mix is boiling, set the heat to low, and let the contents cook for 90 mins.

Step 2

Set your oven to 300 degrees before doing anything else.

Step 3

Now place one C. of the liquid to the side and remove the rest.

Step 4

Get a bowl, combine: 1/4 C. of olive oil, eggplant, and garlic.

Step 5

Stir the mix to evenly coat everything then place the mix into a casserole dish. Cook the eggplants in the oven for 50 mins then add the chilies to the dish and keep cooking the mix for 12 more mins.

Step 6

Remove the insides of your eggplant and place them into the bowl of a food processor. Combine in the 3 tsp of the reserved liquid, garlic and chilies, 2 tbsp olive oil, cumin, harissa, and chickpeas.

Step 7

Process the mix into a smooth paste and add in some more of the reserved liquid if needed. The mix should be creamy.

Step 8

Serve the mix with some toasted pita rounds.

Step 9

Enjoy.

NORTH AFRICAN BREAKFAST

Prep Time: 15 mins- **Total Time:** 45 mins

SERVINGS: 6

NUTRITIONALS VALUE

Calories 178.2, Cholesterol 310.0mg, Sodium 366.3mg, Carbohydrates 9.3g, Protein 11.6g

INGREDIENTS

- 1 lb carrot, sliced
- 1/4 C. fresh flat-leaf parsley, chopped
- 1 tbsp caraway seed, freshly ground
- 1 tbsp extra virgin olive oil
- 1 tbsp harissa, see appendix
- 4 large garlic cloves, diced
- 1/2 tsp salt
- pepper, freshly ground
- 8 large eggs, fresh
- 2 eggs, hard cooked and finely chopped

DIRECTIONS

Step 1

Get your oven's broiler hot and begin to steam your carrots over 2 inches of boiling water, with a steamer insert, for 25 mins, with a lid on the pot.

Step 2

Add the carrots to the bowl of a food processor and begin to puree them, combine in some pepper, some salt, caraway, garlic, and the harissa.

Step 3

Continue to puree the mix until it is smooth.

Step 4

Get a bowl, combine: 1/2 tsp salt and the eggs.

Step 5

Whisk the eggs evenly then add in the carrot mix and hard boiled eggs.

Step 6

Stir the mix again then add in the parsley.

Step 7

Get your olive oil hot then begin to fry the egg mix for 5 mins then place everything under the broiler for 5 more mins.

Step 8

Enjoy.

CLASSICAL LENTILS

Prep Time: 15 mins- **Total Time:** 6 hrs 15 mins

SERVINGS: 6

NUTRITIONALS VALUE

Calories 111.8, Cholesterol 0.0mg, Sodium 34.8mg, Carbohydrates 6.7g, Protein 1.4g

INGREDIENTS

- 2 large onions, diced
- 2 can chopped tomatoes with juice
- 2 large carrots, peeled and diced
- 2 C. vegetable stock
- 2 celery ribs, diced
- 2 cans red kidney beans, rinsed and drained
- 1 tbsp oil
- 2 tbsps concentrated tomato paste
- 3 garlic cloves, finely chopped

- salt
- 1 1/2 C. green lentils
- ground black pepper
- 3 small red chilies
- 1 tsp harissa, see appendix
- 1 tsp ground cumin

DIRECTIONS

Step 1

Begin to stir fry your carrots, onions, and celery, in oil for 10 mins then combine in the chili, garlic, harissa, and cumin.

Step 2

Let the mix continue to cook for 60 secs then combine in the stock, lentils, tomato paste, and chopped tomatoes.

Step 3

Get the mix boiling, set the heat to low, and let everything gently cook for 10 mins.

Step 4

Now place the mix into the crock pot of a slow cooker and place a lid on the crock pot.

Step 5

Let the content cook for 7 hrs with low level of heat.

Step 6

When 1 hour is left of cooking time add in your kidney beans some pepper and salt.

Step 7

Enjoy.

HARISSA CRAB BAKE

Prep Time: 40 mins- **Total Time:** 1 hr 15 mins

SERVINGS: 8

NUTRITIONALS VALUE

Calories 533.6, Cholesterol 102.0mg, Sodium 1051.5mg, Carbohydrates 60.2g, Protein 32.7g

INGREDIENTS

- 1 1/2 lbs lump crabmeat, picked over
- 1 tsp dried oregano
- 8 C. day-old white bread, cubes
- 1 tsp sweet paprika
- 3 C. warm water
- salt and pepper
- 3 tbsps butter
- 2 C. milk
- 1 onion, diced small
- 1/4 C. heavy cream
- 1 red bell pepper, diced small
- 1/2 C. dry white wine
- 3 medium carrots, peeled and coarsely
- 1 1/2 tbsps harissa, see appendix
- grated
- 2/3 C. fresh parmesan cheese, grated
- 3 garlic cloves, diced
- 1 tsp ground cumin

DIRECTIONS

Step 1

Get a bowl, combine: water and the pieces of bread. Leave the mix for 30 mins. Squeeze the bread together to remove all the liquids then break it into pieces. Set your oven to 375 degrees before doing anything else. Now get your butter hot and begin to stir fry your bell pepper and onions for 5 mins in the butter.

Step 2

Now combine in the pepper, carrots, salt, cumin, garlic, paprika, and oregano. Stir fry everything for 60 more secs then combine in the wine, bread, cream, and milk. Continue to fry everything for 7 more mins then combine in the crab, stir the mix, then shut the heat.

Step 3

Top everything with the harissa, some pepper and salt as well.

Step 4

Then place the mix in a casserole dish.

Step 5

Cover everything with the cheese and cook the dish in the oven for 22 mins. Enjoy.

MASHED POTATO ALTERNATIVE OF PARSNIPS WITH CARROTS I

Prep Time: 15 mins- **Total Time:** 35 mins

SERVINGS: 4

NUTRITIONALS VALUE

Calories

164 kcal, Fat

17.4 g, Carbohydrates 2.7g, Protein < 0.5 g, Cholesterol 46 mg, Sodium 220 mg

INGREDIENTS

- 8 parsnips, peeled and cut into 2 inch
- 6 tbsp butter, divided
- pieces
- sea salt and freshly ground black pepper
- 2 carrots, peeled and cut into 2-inch
- to taste
- pieces
- 1/4 C. snipped chives

DIRECTIONS

Step 1

In large pan, place the parsnips, carrots and enough salted water to cover the vegetables.

Step 2

Bring to a boil over high heat.

Step 3

Reduce the heat to medium-low and simmer, covered for about 15-20 minutes.

Step 4

Drain well and return vegetables to pan on low heat.

Step 5

Stir in the chives and 3 tbsp of the butter.

Step 6

With an immersion blender, puree the mixture.

Step 7

Add 3 tbsp of the butter and blend till mixture becomes smooth.

Step 8

Season with the salt and pepper to taste.

MASHED POTATO ALTERNATIVE II

Prep Time: 10 mins- **Total Time:** 40 mins

SERVINGS: 8

NUTRITIONALS VALUE

Calories 143 kcal, Fat 10.7 g, Carbohydrates 7.1g, Protein 5 g, Cholesterol 31 mg, Sodium 441 mg

INGREDIENTS

- 5 C. whole milk
- 1/2 tsp ground black pepper
- 10 parsnips, peeled and cubed
- salt or to taste
- 1 tsp salt
- 1/4 C. butter
- 1 tsp dried thyme

DIRECTIONS

Step 1

In a large pan, heat the milk on medium heat till warmed and just under a boil.

Step 2

Stir in the parsnips and 1 tsp of the salt and cook, covered for about 25-30 minutes.

Step 3

Drain the parsnips, reserving the warm milk in a bowl.

Step 4

In the same pan, add the parsnips, 1 C. of the reserved warm milk, butter, thyme and pepper and with a hand mixer, blend till smooth.

Step 5

Add more milk, salt or pepper as desired.

JAPANESE TERIYAKI PARSNIPS

Prep Time: 5 mins Total Time : 30 mins

SERVINGS: 4

NUTRITIONALS VALUE

Calories 143 kcal, Fat 3.2 g, Carbohydrates 28.1g, Protein 1.9 g, Cholesterol 8 mg, Sodium 377 mg

INGREDIENTS

- 1 lb. parsnips, peeled
- 2 tbsp teriyaki sauce
- 1 tbsp butter
- 2 tbsp white sugar

DIRECTIONS

Step 1

In large pan, place the parsnips and enough water to cover and bring to a boil over high heat.

Step 2

Reduce the heat to medium-low and simmer for about 15 minutes.

Step 3

Drain well and keep aside to cool slightly.

Step 4

Cut the parsnips into 2 1/2-inch sticks.

Step 5

In a skillet, melt the butter on medium heat.

Step 6

Stir in the sugar and parsnips and toss to coat.

Step 7

Add the teriyaki sauce and cook for about 5 minutes.

PARSNIP BURGERS

Prep Time: 15 mins- **Total Time:** 45 mins

SERVINGS: 8

NUTRITIONALS VALUE

Calories 167 kcal, Fat 9.5 g, Carbohydrates 18.4g, Protein 2.9 g, Cholesterol 10 mg, Sodium 137 mg

INGREDIENTS

- 1 lb. parsnips, peeled and chopped
- 1/2 C. bread crumbs
- 2 tbsp butter
- salt and ground black pepper to taste
- 1/2 small onion, finely chopped
- 2 C. vegetable oil for frying
- 2 tbsp all-purpose flour
- 1 C. milk

DIRECTIONS

Step 1

In large pan, place the parsnips and enough water to cover and bring to a boil. Cook for about 10 minutes.

Step 2

Drain the parsnips and with a potato masher, mash them.

Step 3

Transfer into a bowl and keep aside.

Step 4

In a pan, melt the butter on medium heat.

Step 5

Stir in the onions and cook for about 5 minutes.

Step 6

Add the flour, beating continuously till the mixture becomes paste-like.

Step 7

Slowly, add the milk into the flour mixture, beating continuously and bring to a simmer over medium heat.

Step 8

Cook, stirring continuously for about 10 minutes.

Step 9

Transfer the sauce in the bowl of the mashed parsnips.'

Step 10

Add the bread crumbs, salt and pepper and mix well.

Step 11

Make equal sized patties rom the mixture.

Step 12

In a large, deep skillet, heat the oil to 350 degrees F and fry the patties or about 5 minutes, turning once.

Step 13

Transfer the patties onto a paper towel lined plate to drain.

Step 14

Serve hot.

POTATO CHIP ALTERNATIVE WITH PARSNIPS

Prep Time: 30 mins **Total Time** : 1 hr

SERVINGS: 4

NUTRITIONALS VALUE

Calories 362 kcal, Fat 23.1 g, Carbohydrates 37.3g, Protein 3.4 g, Cholesterol 31 mg, Sodium 243 mg

INGREDIENTS

- 4 parsnips
- salt
- 1/4 C. butter, melted
- chili powder
- 1/2 C. all-purpose flour
- cayenne pepper
- 2 C. vegetable oil for frying

DIRECTIONS

Step 1

Peel the parsnips and slice into 1/4-inch rounds.

Step 2

In a pan of lightly salted boiling water, add parsnips and cook for about 5 minutes.

Step 3

Drain and keep aside to cool slightly.

Step 4

Coat the parsnip slices in the melted butter and arrange onto a baking sheet.

Step 5

Refrigerate for about 30 minutes.

Step 6

Remove from the refrigerator and coat parsnip slices in flour.

Step 7

In a large heavy skillet, heat the oil on medium-high heat and fry the parsnip slices till golden brown from both sides.

Step 8

Transfer the slices onto a paper towel lined plate to drain.

Step 9

Sprinkle with the salt, chili powder and cayenne and serve.

RUSTIC OAK WOOD SOUP

Prep Time: 25 mins- **Total Time:** 1 hr 30 mins

SERVINGS: 10

NUTRITIONALS VALUE

Calories 187 kcal, Fat 9.7 g, Carbohydrates 23.9g, Protein 2.9 g, Cholesterol 22 mg, Sodium 361 mg

INGREDIENTS

- 2 lb. parsnips, peeled and cut into 1/2 inch 1 tsp ground ginger pieces
- 1/2 tsp ground cardamom
- 3 carrots, peeled and cut into 1/2-inch
- 1/2 tsp ground allspice
- pieces
- 1/2 tsp ground nutmeg
- 1 tbsp olive oil
- 1/4 tsp cayenne pepper
- sea salt and ground black pepper to taste
- 4 C. chicken stock
- 1 tbsp olive oil
- 1 C. whole milk
- 1 large onion, diced
- 1/2 C. heavy cream
- 3 stalks celery, diced
- 1 tbsp butter
- 3 cloves garlic, minced
- 1 tbsp brown sugar

DIRECTIONS

Step 1

Set your oven to 425 degrees F before doing anything else.

Step 2

In a bowl, pace the parsnips, carrots, 1 tbsp the olive oil, salt and pepper and toss to coat.

Step 3

Place the vegetables onto baking sheet evenly.

Step 4

Cook in the oven for about 30 minutes.

Step 5

In a large pan, heat the remaining 1 tbsp of the olive oil on medium heat and sauté the onion and celery for about 7 minutes.

Step 6

Reduce the heat to low and stir in the butter, garlic, brown sugar and the roasted parsnips and carrots and cook for about 10 minutes.

Step 7

Stir in the ginger, cardamom, allspice, nutmeg and cayenne pepper and cook for about 1 minute.

Step 8

Add the chicken stock and bring to a boil on medium-high heat.

Step 9

Reduce the heat to medium-low and simmer, partially covered for about 15 minutes.

Step 10

Remove from the heat and keep aside to cool slightly.

Step 11

In a blender, add the soup in batches and pulse till smooth.

Step 12

Return the soup into a pan on medium-low heat.

Step 13

Stir in the milk, cream, salt and pepper before serving.

NEW ENGLAND STYLE CHOWDER

Prep Time: 20 mins- **Total Time:** 50 mins

SERVINGS: 7

NUTRITIONALS VALUE

Calories 348 kcal, Fat 19.2 g, Carbohydrates 22.2g, Protein 22.8 g, Cholesterol 101 mg, Sodium 437 mg

INGREDIENTS

- 1 lb. cod fillets
- 1 onion, chopped
- 1/2 lb. lightly smoked cod, skin and bones 1 C. milk removed
- 1 C. heavy whipping cream
- 1/2 lemon
- salt to taste
- 1 sprig fresh thyme
- ground black pepper to taste
- 1 lb. parsnip, chopped
- 1/2 lb. potatoes
- 3 tbsp butter

DIRECTIONS

Step 1

If the smoked cod has a strong smoky flavor, soak it in water for about 30 minutes.

Step 2

Drain well and rinse.

Step 3

In a large pan, add the cod, smoked cod, 1 tbsp. of lemon juice, thyme and enough water to cover and bring to a gentle simmer.

Step 4

Poach the fish for about 8-10 minutes.

Step 5

Transfer the fish into a bowl, reserving the poaching liquid.

Step 6

Keep aside the fish to cool.

Step 7

Now, break the cod it into large bite-sized pieces and keep aside.

Step 8

Meanwhile peel the parsnips and cut into 1/4-inch thick slices.

Step 9

Peel the potatoes and cut into 1/2-inch cubes.

Step 10

In a bowl of water, place the potatoes to prevent discoloring.

Step 11

In a large pan, melt 2 tbsp of the butter on medium heat and sauté the onion till golden.

Step 12

Add the parsnips, potatoes and 3 C. of the reserved poaching liquid and bring to a boil.

Step 13

Reduce the heat and simmer, covered for about 15 minutes.

Step 14

In a small pan, heat the milk and cream but do not boil.

Step 15

Add the milk mixture into the vegetable mixture and stir to combine.

Step 16

Stir in the cod, smoked cod, salt and freshly ground pepper.

Step 17

Just before serving stir in the remaining butter.

Step 18

Serve with a topping of the chives.

NOVEMBER'S VEGGIES

Prep Time: 20 mins- **Total Time:** 35 mins

SERVINGS: 8

NUTRITIONALS VALUE

Calories 163 kcal, Fat 6.3 g, Carbohydrates 26.7g, Protein 2 g, Cholesterol 15 mg, Sodium 190 mg

INGREDIENTS

- 1/4 C. butter
- 3/4 C. chicken stock
- 4 large carrots, cut into 3-inch x 1/2-
- 2 tbsp lemon juice
- inch pieces

- salt and ground black pepper to taste
- 4 large parsnips, cut into 3-inch x 1/2-
- 3 tbsp chopped fresh chives
- inch pieces
- 3/4 C. orange juice

DIRECTIONS

Step 1

In a large skillet, melt the butter on medium heat and stir fry the carrots and parsnips for about 8-10 minutes.

Step 2

Stir in the orange juice, chicken stock, lemon juice, salt and black pepper and bring to a boil.

Step 3

Reduce the heat to low and simmer, covered for about 10 minutes, stirring occasionally.

Step 4

Season with more salt and black pepper if required.

Step 5

Serve with a topping of the chives.

HUNGRY BEE PARSNIPS

Prep Time: 10 mins Total Time : 40 mins

SERVINGS: 6

NUTRITIONALS VALUE

Calories 190 kcal, Fat 2.3 g, Carbohydrates 44.3g, Protein 1.5 g, Cholesterol 5 mg, Sodium 27 mg

INGREDIENTS

- 1/2 C. warm water
- 5 parsnips, peeled and cubed
- 1/2 C. honey
- 1 tbsp melted butter

DIRECTIONS

Step 1

Set your oven to 375 degrees F before doing anything else.

Step 2

In a large bowl, add the water, butter, and honey and mix till the honey is dissolved.

Step 3

Add the parsnips and toss to coat.

Step 4

Transfer the parsnips mixture into a 12x9-inch glass baking dish **Step 5**

Cook in the oven for about 30 minutes.

BALSAMIC PARSNIPS AND BRUSSELS SPROUTS

Prep Time: 15 mins- **Total Time:** 55 mins

SERVINGS: 4

NUTRITIONALS VALUE

Calories 222 kcal, Fat 6.7 g, Carbohydrates 39.6g, Protein 5.6 g, Cholesterol 0 mg, Sodium 276 mg

INGREDIENTS

- 1/3 C. balsamic vinaigrette salad dressing

- 1 lb. parsnips, peeled
- (such as Kraft(R))
- 1 large red onion, thickly sliced
- 1 tbsp brown sugar
- 1 tbsp chopped fresh thyme
- 1 lb. Brussels sprouts, halved

DIRECTIONS

Step 1

Set your oven to 400 degrees F before doing anything else.

Step 2

In a bowl, mix together the salad dressing, brown sugar and thyme.

Step 3

In a 13x9-inch baking dish, add the Brussels sprouts, parsnips, red onion and dressing mixture and toss to coat.

Step 4

Cook in the oven for about 40 minutes.

HOW TO COOK PARSNIPS

Prep Time: 10 mins Total Time : 40 mins

SERVINGS: 4

NUTRITIONALS VALUE

Calories 111 kcal, Fat 3.2 g, Carbohydrates 20.6g, Protein 1.4 g, Cholesterol 8 mg, Sodium 32 mg

INGREDIENTS

- 1 lb. parsnips, peeled, cut in half

- 1 pinch salt
- crosswise, and cut into narrow strips
- ground black pepper to taste
- lengthwise
- 1 tbsp butter

DIRECTIONS

Step 1

In large pan, place the parsnips and enough water to cover and bring to a boil over high heat.

Step 2

Reduce the heat and simmer for about 15-20 minutes.

Step 3

Drain well and pat dry with a paper towel.

Step 4

Keep aside to cool slightly.

Step 5

In a skillet, melt the butter on medium heat.

Step 6

Arrange the parsnips into the hot butter in an even layer.

Step 7

Sprinkle the parsnips with the salt and black pepper and cook for about 5-8 minutes per side.

PENNSYLVANIA FREEWAY PARSNIPS

Prep Time: 15 mins- **Total Time:** 1 hr

SERVINGS: 6

NUTRITIONALS VALUE

Calories 404 kcal, Fat 23.8 g, Carbohydrates 46.6g, Protein 3.7 g, Cholesterol 64 mg, Sodium 643 mg

INGREDIENTS

- 3 lb. parsnips, peeled and cut into 1/2-
- 1 tsp salt
- inch pieces
- 1 tsp white sugar
- 1/4 lb. butter, melted
- 1/4 C. bread crumbs
- 1/4 C. sherry
- 2 tbsp butter, cut into small pieces
- 1/4 C. heavy whipping cream

DIRECTIONS

Step 1

In a large pan, add the parsnips and enough water to cover and bring to a boil.

Step 2

Reduce heat to medium-low and simmer for about 20-30 minutes.

Step 3

Drain well and keep aside to cool slightly.

Step 4

Set your oven to 350 degrees F.

Step 5

In a bowl, add the parsnips, melted butter, sherry, heavy whipping cream, salt and white sugar and beat till smooth.

Step 6

Place the mixture into a baking dish and top with the bread crumbs evenly.

Step 7

Place the butter on top in the form of dots.

Step 8

Cook in the oven for about 25-30 minutes.

FRIGID WINTER SOUP

Prep Time: 35 mins Total Time : 55 mins

SERVINGS: 30

NUTRITIONALS VALUE

Calories 92 kcal, Fat 5.3 g, Carbohydrates 9.7g, Protein 1.5 g, Cholesterol 2 mg, Sodium < 344 mg

INGREDIENTS

- 1/3 C. extra-virgin olive oil
- 2 C. fresh shiitake mushrooms, sliced
- 2 large carrots, peeled and chopped
- 1/3 C. extra-virgin olive oil
- 2 celery ribs, chopped
- 5 cloves garlic, minced
- 1 white onion, peeled and chopped
- 1 bunch fresh tarragon
- 3 large Portobello mushroom caps,

- 3 sprigs fresh thyme
- cleaned and chopped
- kosher salt to taste (optional)
- 5 (13.75 oz.) cans chicken broth
- 8 parsnips, peeled and chopped

DIRECTIONS

Step 1

In a deep pan, heat 1/3 C. of the olive oil on medium heat and sauté the carrots, celery, and onion for about 5 minutes.

Step 2

Stir in the Portobello mushrooms and cook for about 5 minutes.

Step 3

Add the chicken broth, parsnips and shiitake mushrooms and bring to a boil.

Step 4

Reduce the heat to medium and simmer for about 10 minutes.

Step 5

Remove from the heat.

Step 6

In a blender, place 1/3 C. of the olive oil, garlic, tarragon and thyme and pulse till well combined.

Step 7

Stir the mixture into the soup with the kosher salt.

TUESDAY'S PANCAKES

Prep Time: 10 mins- **Total Time:** 25 mins

SERVINGS: 2

NUTRITIONALS VALUE

Calories 194 kcal, Fat 13 g, Carbohydrates 14.7g, Protein 5.8 g, Cholesterol 138 mg, Sodium 641 mg

INGREDIENTS

- 1 C. grated peeled parsnips
- 1/2 tsp dried rosemary
- 2 small eggs
- ground black pepper to taste (optional)
- 1/4 C. finely chopped onion
- 1 tsp sunflower oil
- 1 tbsp olive oil
- 1/2 tsp salt

DIRECTIONS

Step 1

In a bowl, add the parsnips, eggs, onion, olive oil, salt, rosemary and black pepper and mix till well combined and lumpy.

Step 2

In a heavy frying pan, heat the sunflower oil on medium heat.

Step 3

With a spoon, place the mixture into the oil and fry for about 6-7 minutes per side.

APPLE DIJON VEGGIE ROAST

Prep Time: 20 mins **Total Time** : 1 hr

SERVINGS: 8

NUTRITIONALS VALUE

Calories 161 kcal, Fat 4.1 g, Carbohydrates 31.2g, Protein 2 g, Cholesterol 0 mg, Sodium 211 mg

INGREDIENTS

- 2/3 C. apple cider
- 1 1/2 lb. carrots, peeled and cut into
- 2 tbsp olive oil
- sticks
- 2 tbsp apple cider vinegar
- 1 1/2 lb. parsnips, peeled and cut into
- 2 tbsp coarse-grain Dijon mustard
- sticks
- 2 tbsp honey
- Aluminum foil
- 2 tsp chopped fresh thyme
- 1/4 tsp salt

DIRECTIONS

Step 1

Set your oven to 400 degrees F before doing anything else and line a roasting pan with a piece of foil.

Step 2

In a very large bowl, add the apple cider, oil, vinegar, mustard, honey, thyme and salt and beat till well combined.

Step 3

Add the carrots and parsnips and toss to coat.

Step 4

Place the vegetables mixture onto the prepared roasting pan in an even layer.

Step 5

Cook in the oven for about 35 minutes, stirring twice.

A COUNTRY DINNER

Prep Time: 15 mins- **Total Time:** 1 hr

SERVINGS: 6

NUTRITIONALS VALUE

Calories 212 kcal, Fat 16 g, Carbohydrates 12.9g, Protein 6.2 g, Cholesterol 55 mg, Sodium 332 mg

INGREDIENTS

- 3 Yukon Gold potatoes, peeled
- 2 oz. finely grated Parmigiano-Reggiano
- 2 parsnips, peeled
- cheese, divided
- 2 cloves garlic, minced
- 3/4 C. crème fraiche, divided
- 1 tbsp butter, melted
- 1 C. chicken broth
- salt and ground black pepper to taste
- 1 pinch cayenne pepper
- 1 tsp fresh thyme leaves, divided

DIRECTIONS

Step 1

Set your oven to 375 degrees F before doing anything else.

Step 2

In a large bowl, of cold water, place the potatoes and parsnips.

Step 3

In a large baking dish, spread the garlic and melted butter evenly.

Step 4

With a mandolin slicer, slice the potatoes very thinly.

Step 5

With a vegetable peeler, slice the parsnips thinly.

Step 6

In the bottom of the prepared baking dish, place 1/3 of the potato slices and sprinkle with the salt and black pepper, followed by a few thyme leaves and a light dusting of Parmigiano-Reggiano cheese. Top with about 3 tbsp of the crème fraiche.

Step 7

Arrange 1/2 of the parsnip slices over the crème fraiche in an even layer and sprinkle with the salt and black pepper.

Step 8

Repeat the layering process as 1/3 potato slices, salt, black pepper, thyme, Parmigiano-Reggiano cheese, crème fraiche, and remaining 1/2 parsnip slices.

Step 9

Sprinkle with the salt. Top with remaining 1/3 of the potato slices and sprinkle with the salt.Slowly, place the chicken broth, about 3 tbsp at a time.

Step 10

Shake the dish gently to eliminate air bubbles.

Step 11

Gently spread the remaining 2 tbsp crème fraiche over the potatoes.

Step 12

Sprinkle cayenne and remaining Parmigiano-Reggiano cheese over the top.

Step 13

Cook in the oven for about 45-60 minutes.

MASHED POTATO ALTERNATIVE

Prep Time: 5 minsTotal Time : 15 mins

SERVINGS: 2

NUTRITIONALS VALUE

Calories 130.1, Fat 6.7g, Cholesterol 17.4mg, Sodium 86.9mg, Carbohydrates 16.4g, Protein 2.8g

INGREDIENTS

- 1 whole rutabaga
- salt
- 1 oz. milk
- pepper
- 1 tbsp butter

DIRECTIONS

Step 1

Peel and cube the rutabaga.

Step 2

In a pan of boiling water, cook the rutabaga for about 40 minutes.

Step 3

Drain and return to the dry pan on low heat to allow the excess water to evaporate off.

Step 4

Add a little milk, a lot of butter, some salt and plenty of freshly ground black pepper and mash well.

5-INGREDIENT ROOTS

Prep Time: 7 mins- **Total Time:** 27 mins

SERVINGS: 4

NUTRITIONALS VALUE

Calories 63.9, Fat 3.0g, Cholesterol 7.6mg, Sodium 44.7mg, Carbohydrates 8.7g, Protein 1.2g

INGREDIENTS

- 1 medium rutabaga, peeled, diced 1/2 inch 1 tbsp butter dice
- salt & pepper
- 1/4 tsp ground ginger
- 2 tbsp fresh orange juice

DIRECTIONS

Step 1

In a pan of boiling water, add the rutabaga and cook, covered for about 20 minutes.

Step 2

Drain and Mash completely.

Step 3

Stir in the remaining ingredients and serve hot.

SWEET RUTABAGAS EUROLAND

Prep Time: 10 mins **Total Time** : 40 mins

SERVINGS: 1

NUTRITIONALS VALUE

Calories 238.3, Fat 23.0g, Cholesterol 61.0mg, Sodium 167.1mg, Carbohydrates 8.9g, Protein 0.2g

INGREDIENTS

- 1 small rutabaga
- salt and pepper
- 2 tbsp butter
- 2 tsp brown sugar

DIRECTIONS

Step 1

Peel the rutabaga and cut it into 1/2-inch sized cubes.

Step 2

In a heavy skillet, melt the butter on medium heat and sauté the rutabaga cubes till browned from all sides, stirring occasionally.

Step 3

Add the sugar and reduce the heat to low.

Step 4

Cook, covered for about 20-30 minutes, stirring occasionally.

Step 5

Stir in the salt and pepper and serve.

COUNTRY WAGON STEW

Prep Time: 5 mins- **Total Time:** 48 mins

SERVINGS: 4

NUTRITIONALS VALUE

Calories 281.8, Fat 11.2g, Cholesterol 109.7mg, Sodium 693.0mg, Carbohydrates 17.1g, Protein 27.0g

INGREDIENTS

- 1 small rutabaga, peeled and diced in
- 1/3 C. flour
- 1/2-inch pieces
- 1/4 tsp salt
- 2 medium parsnips, peeled and diced in
- 1/4 tsp pepper
- 1/2-inch pieces
- 1 large leek, chopped
- 1 medium carrot, peeled and diced in
- 2 C. chicken broth
- 1/2-inch pieces
- 2 tbsp chopped fresh Italian parsley, chopped 2 tbsp butter
- 1 lb. boneless skinless chicken thighs, cut
- into bite-size pieces

DIRECTIONS

Step 1

In a large pan of lightly salted boiling water, add the rutabaga, parsnips and carrot and cook, covered for about 10 minutes.

Step 2

Drain well and keep aside.

Step 3

Sprinkle the chicken with flour, salt and pepper, reserving any leftover flour.

Step 4

Meanwhile in a large pan, melt the butter on medium heat and sear the chicken in 2 batches till browned.

Step 5

Transfer the chicken into a bowl.

Step 6

In the same pan, add the leek and sauté for about 3 minutes.

Step 7

Add 1 tbsp of the reserved flour and stir till a paste forms.

Step 8

Stir in the chicken broth and bring to a boil, stirring occasionally.

Step 9

Add the chicken, vegetables and reduce the heat to low.

Step 10

Simmer, covered for about 10 minutes.

Step 11

Serve with a sprinkling of the chopped parsley.

EASY IRISH DINNER

Prep Time: 30 mins **Total Time** : 3 hrs 30 mins

SERVINGS: 6

NUTRITIONALS VALUE

Calories 918.2, Fat 44.2g, Cholesterol 222.1mg, Sodium 3837.8mg, Carbohydrates 83.0g, Protein 48.6g

INGREDIENTS

- 1 (3 lb.) corned beef brisket
- 1/2 C. light brown sugar
- 1 head cabbage
- 1 tbsp mustard seeds
- 2 large onions
- 1 tbsp kosher salt
- 1 1/2 lb. small red potatoes
- 1 tsp fresh ground black pepper
- 4 carrots
- 2 parsnips
- 1 (2 lb.) rutabagas
- 3 C. unsweetened apple juice

DIRECTIONS

Step 1

In a large pan, add the beef, 3 C. of the apple juice and enough cold water to cover the beef and bring to a boil on high heat.

Step 2

Add 1/2 C. of the brown sugar and mustard seeds and again bring to a boil, skimming off any fat from the top surface.

Step 3

Reduce the heat and simmer, covered for about 2 hours.

Step 4

Cut some wedges off the cabbage.

Step 5

Peel the carrots and cut into chunks.

Step 6

Peel the parsnips and cut into chunks.

Step 7

Peel a couple of onions but leave the root end on.

Step 8

Cut the onions in half through the root end, then in half again, through the root end.

Step 9

Peel the rutabaga and cut into chunks.

Step 10

In the pan of beef, add all the vegetables except the cabbage and increase the heat to high.

Step 11

Bring to a boil and stir in the kosher salt and black pepper.

Step 12

Add half of the apple juice and half of the water and bring to a boil.

Step 13

Reduce the heat and simmer, covered for about 15 minutes.

Step 14

Uncover and stir in the cabbage.

Step 15

Increase the heat to high and bring to a boil.

Step 16

Reduce the heat and simmer for about 20-25 minutes.

Step 17

Transfer the corned beef onto a chopping board and carve it.

Step 18

Transfer the carved beef into a platter.

Step 19

Transfer the vegetables into another platter and serve alongside the salt, pepper and butter.

LEEK, CELERY, AND TOMATO SOUP

Prep Time: 20 mins **Total Time** : 1 hr 10 mins

SERVINGS: 6

NUTRITIONALS VALUE

Calories 157.5, Fat 2.8g, Cholesterol 0.0mg, Sodium 367.0mg, Carbohydrates 31.9g, Protein 3.9g

INGREDIENTS

- 1 tbsp olive oil
- 2 C. peeled russet potatoes, 1/2-inch
- 1 1/2 C. chopped leeks (white and pale
- pieces
- green parts only)
- 2 C. carrots, sliced

- 1/2 C. chopped celery
- 1 (28 oz.) cans diced tomatoes with juice
- 1 garlic clove, minced
- 4 (14 1/2 oz.) cans vegetable broth or 4
- 2 C. peeled turnips, 1/2-inch pieces
- (14 1/2 oz.) cans low chicken broth
- 2 C. peeled rutabagas, 1/2-inch pieces

DIRECTIONS

Step 1

In a heavy large pan, heat the oil on medium-low heat and sauté the leek, celery and garlic for about 5 minutes.

Step 2

Add the turnips, rutabagas, potatoes, carrots, tomatoes with juices and 2 cans of the broth and bring to a boil.

Step 3

Reduce the heat and simmer, covered for about 45 minutes.

Step 4

Transfer about 4 C. of the soup into a food processor and pulse till almost smooth.

Step 5

Return the pureed soup to the pan.

Step 6

Add the remaining 2 cans of the broth and bring to a simmer.

Step 7

Season with the salt and pepper and serve.

FEBRUARY VEGGIE COMBO

Prep Time: 20 mins- **Total Time:** 45 mins

SERVINGS: 4

NUTRITIONALS VALUE

Calories 274.0, Fat 23.8g, Cholesterol 61.3mg, Sodium 781.7mg, Carbohydrates 14.2g, Protein 3.3g

INGREDIENTS

- 1 C. chopped turnip
- 3 C. water
- 2 C. chopped rutabagas
- 1/4 lb. butter
- 1/2 C. chopped carrot
- 2 tbsp chicken-flavored broth
- 1 C. chopped broccoli
- 2 tbsp Mrs. Dash seasoning mix, blend
- 1 C. Brussels sprout

DIRECTIONS

Step 1

Peel and chop the turnips, rutabaga and carrots and cut into bite sized pieces.

Step 2

Trim the Brussels sprout and remove the damaged leaves.

Step 3

Chop the crowns of broccoli and then chop the stems.

Step 4

In the bottom of a large colander, place the turnips and rutabaga, followed by the carrots, Brussels sprout and broccoli.

Step 5

In a 3 quart pan, mix together about 4 C. of the water and 2 tbsp of the Soup Base.

Step 6

Arrange the colander in the pan of water.

Step 7

Sprinkle the vegetable mixture with Mrs. Dash seasoning and top with the butter.

Step 8

Cover the pan, setting the lid slightly off-center to vent your steam and bring to a boil.

Step 9

Reduce the heat to medium-high and steam for about 20-25 minutes.

POT ROAST SKILLET

Prep Time: 20 mins- **Total Time:** 3 hrs 20 mins

SERVINGS: 8

NUTRITIONALS VALUE

Calories 531.5, Fat 31.4g, Cholesterol 115.6mg, Sodium 228.8mg, Carbohydrates 26.2g, Protein 34.6g

INGREDIENTS

- 3 lb. pot roast, as round as you can find
- 1 dozen button mushroom
- 1 tbsp McCormick's Montreal Brand
- Sauce:

- steak seasoning
- 2 tsp beef base
- 4 potatoes, scrubbed and peeled and
- 2 tsp mushrooms, base
- quartered
- 1 C. tomato juice
- 1 turnip, scrubbed and pared
- 1 sprig thyme
- 1/2 onion, sliced in big chunks
- parsley (to garnish)
- 2 C. carrots, pared (and chunked)
- 1 C. rutabaga, diced
- 1 celery rib, peeled (and chunked)

DIRECTIONS

Step 1

Set your oven to 375 degrees F before doing anything else.

Step 2

Season the roast with steak seasoning evenly.

Step 3

Heat a cast iron pan and sear the roast till browned completely.

Step 4

Add the remaining ingredients and stir to combine.

Step 5

In a bowl, mix together all the sauce ingredients. With 1 C. of boiling water. Pour the sauce mixture over the roast mixture evenly.

Step 6

Cover the pan tightly and cook in the oven for about 3 hours.

Step 7

Transfer the meat and veggies into a warm platter.

Step 8

Thicken the sauce according to your liking.

Step 9

Serve the meat mixture with a sprinkling of the parsley alongside the sauce.

PARISIAN VEGGIE BAKE

Prep Time: 1 hr- **Total Time:** 2 hrs 15 mins

SERVINGS: 4

NUTRITIONALS VALUE

Calories 220.6, Fat 1.2g, Cholesterol 0.0mg, Sodium 1234.5mg, Carbohydrates 49.0g, Protein 9.4g

INGREDIENTS

- 3 large white potatoes
- 1 (8 oz.) cans tomato sauce
- 1/2 medium brown onion
- 1 tsp beef bouillon powder
- 2 -3 large carrots, peeled
- 8 oz. water
- 1 large rutabaga, peeled

- 2 tbsp pepper
- 2 large zucchini
- 1 tsp salt
- 12 oz. sliced mushrooms
- 1 tsp onion powder
- 1 green bell pepper, seeded and stemmed
- 1 tsp crushed basil
- 3 garlic cloves
- 1 bay leaf
- 2 beefsteak tomatoes
- 1 lb. thin cut beef (optional)

DIRECTIONS

Step 1

Set your oven to 350 degrees F before doing anything else.

Step 2

Cut the potatoes, zucchini and bell pepper into 1/4-inch thick slices.

Step 3

Cut the carrots, tomato and rutabaga into 1/8-inch thick slices.

Step 4

Cut the onion thin slices.

Step 5

Cut the beef into 1-1 1/2-inch wide, 2-inch long and n 1/4-inch thick strips.

Step 6

In a baking dish, arrange half of the potato, carrot, onion and bell pepper.

Step 7

Then, arrange half of the rutabaga and sprinkle with about 1 tsp of the pepper.

Step 8

Then, arrange half of the zucchini, mushrooms, beef and tomato and sprinkle with 1/2 tsp of the salt.

Step 9

Repeat the layers.

Step 10

In a medium pan, mix together the tomato sauce, water, bouillon, bay leaf, basil, onion powder, 1 tbsp of the pepper and garlic and bring to a gentle boil, stirring continuously.

Step 11

Remove from the heat and discard the bay leaf.

Step 12

Gently, transfer the sauce mixture over the vegetables evenly.

Step 13

Cover the baking dish and cook in the oven for about 45 minutes.

Step 14

Uncover the baking dish and with the back of a spoon, gently push down the mixture.

Step 15

Cover the baking dish and cook in the oven for about 30 minutes.

COLD WINTER CHOWDER

Prep Time: 15 mins- **Total Time:** 1 hr 15 mins

SERVINGS: 8

NUTRITIONALS VALUE

Calories 423.8, Fat 24.9g, Cholesterol 57.8mg, Sodium 666.2mg, Carbohydrates 40.1g, Protein 14.3g

INGREDIENTS

- 250 ml cooked crumbled turkey bacon
- 2 ml basil
- 1 7/8 liters prepared low chicken broth
- 2 ml marjoram
- 500 ml water
- 250 ml frozen corn
- 750 ml rutabagas
- 500 ml table cream
- 250 ml diced onions
- 2 (420 g) packages dry unprepared roasted
- 500 ml asparagus, cut in 1 inch pieces
- garlic mashed potatoes
- 10 ml chili powder
- 10 ml Cajun seasoning

DIRECTIONS

Step 1

Cut bacon into 1/2-inch pieces.

Step 2

Heat a skillet on medium-high heat and cook the bacon till browned completely.

Step 3

Transfer the bacon onto a paper towel lined plate to drain.

Step 4

In a large pan, add the chicken stock, water, bacon, onion and rutabagas and bring to a boil on medium heat.

Step 5

Cook for about 20 minutes, stirring occasionally.

Step 6

Add the asparagus and seasonings and cook for about 20 minutes, stirring occasionally.

Step 7

Add the corn, cream and potatoes and cook for about 10 minutes, stirring occasionally.

Step 8

Remove from the heat and keep aside for about 5 minutes before serving.

HOMEMADE HARISSA(CLASSICAL TUNISIAN STYLE)

Prep Time: 40 mins- **Total Time:** 1 hr

SERVINGS: 192

NUTRITIONALS VALUE

Calories 10 kcal, Fat 0.3 g, Carbohydrates 1.9g, Protein 0.4 g, Cholesterol 0 m, Sodium 26 mg

INGREDIENTS

- 11 oz. dried red chili peppers, stems
- 1/2 tsp ground coriander seed
- removed, seeds, removed
- 2 tsps salt

- 3/4 C. chopped garlic
- 2 C. caraway seed

DIRECTIONS

Step 1

Let your chilies sit submerged in water for 30 mins then remove the liquids.

Step 2

Now add the following to the bowl of a food processor: salt, pepper, coriander, garlic, and caraway.

Step 3

Puree the mix then place everything into a Mason jar and top the mix with a bit of oil.

Step 4

Place the lid on the jar tightly and put everything in the fridge.

Step 5

Enjoy.

RUTABAGA STEW

Prep Time: 20 mins- **Total Time:** 4 hrs 25 mins

SERVINGS: 15

NUTRITIONALS VALUE

Calories 111 kcal, Fat 2.1 g, Carbohydrates 12.9g, Protein 10.7 g, Cholesterol 23 mg, Sodium 80 mg

INGREDIENTS

- 1 tbsp vegetable oil
- 3 stalks celery, diced
- 1 1/2 lbs chicken, diced

- 1 red onion, diced
- 4 rutabagas, peeled and diced
- water, or to cover
- 4 medium beets, peeled and diced
- 4 carrots, diced

DIRECTIONS

Step 1

Stir fry your chicken in veggie oil for 4 mins.

Step 2

Now combine in: red onions, rutabagas, celery, beets, and carrots. Submerge the contents in some water and get the mix boiling.

Step 3

Once the mix is boiling set the heat to low, and simmer the stew for 4 hrs.

Step 4

Make sure you continue to add some water during the cooking time to keep the veggies simmering.

Step 5

Enjoy.

HONEY RUTABAGA COUSCOUS

Prep Time: 15 mins- **Total Time:** 35 mins

SERVINGS: 6

NUTRITIONALS VALUE

Calories 330 kcal, Fat 12.3 g, Carbohydrates 44.2g, Protein 11.7 g, Cholesterol 0 mg, Sodium 89 mg

INGREDIENTS

- 1 rutabaga, chunked
- 1 tsp dried oregano
- 2 C. water
- 1 tsp dried dill weed
- 1 tbsp vegetable oil
- 1/2 tsp ground black pepper
- 1 1/2 C. couscous
- 1/4 tsp cayenne pepper
- 1/2 C. nutritional yeast
- 1 pinch salt to taste (optional)
- 1/4 C. vegetable oil
- 1/4 C. apple cider vinegar
- 1 1/2 tsps honey
- 1 tsp Italian seasoning

DIRECTIONS

Step 1

Steam your rutabaga over 2 inches of boiling water for 12 mins with a steamer insert.

Step 2

Boil 1 tbsp of veggie oil with 2 C. of water then add in the couscous and shut the heat after placing a lid on the pot.

Step 3

Let this sit for 15 mins before stirring after it has cooled.

Step 4

Get a bowl, combine: cayenne, veggie oil, black pepper, vinegar, dill, honey, oregano, and Italian seasonings.

Step 5

Add the rutabaga, couscous, and some salt to the dressing mix.

Step 6

Toss the contents to coat everything evenly.

Step 7

Enjoy.

RUSSIAN SUMMERTIME SALAD

Prep Time: 15 mins- **Total Time:** 15 mins

SERVINGS: 4

NUTRITIONALS VALUE

Calories 167.7, Fat 13.0g, Cholesterol 0.0mg, Sodium 805.5mg, Carbohydrates 10.3g, Protein 5.4g

INGREDIENTS

- FOR SALAD
- 1 tsp country-style Dijon mustard
- 10 -12 C. salad greens, torn into bite-sized 1 pinch salt pieces
- 1 pinch pepper
- 3/4 C. red radish, cut into 1/16 inch slices 3 tbsp walnut oil
- 1/4 C. green onion, cut into 1/8 inch
- 1 pinch sugar (optional)
- slices

FOR DRESSING

- 1 tbsp cider vinegar
- 1 1/2 tbsp apple juice (juice)

DIRECTIONS

Step 1

In a large bowl, place the salad greens and top with the radish and onions.

Step 2

For the dressing in a bowl, add all the Ingredients except oil and beat till well combined.

Step 3

Slowly, add the oil, beating continuously till well combined.

Step 4

Place the dressing over the salad and toss to coat well.

Step 5

Note: Country-style mustard gets hotter when you prepare the dressing in advance. If you do so, you should consider reducing the amount of mustard used.

AMISH INSPIRED RELISH

Prep Time: 5 mins- **Total Time:** 30 mins

SERVINGS: 12

NUTRITIONALS VALUE

Calories 107.6, Fat 1.5g, Cholesterol 0.0mg, Sodium 126.1mg, Carbohydrates 27.0g, Protein 1.4g

INGREDIENTS

- 1 lb radish, julienned
- 3/4 C. sugar
- 1 medium onion, julienned

- 1/2 tsp salt
- 2 tbsp whole allspice
- 3/4 C. water
- 1/4 tsp whole cloves
- 1 tsp mustard seeds
- 1 C. white vinegar

DIRECTIONS

Step 1

In a bowl, mix together radishes and onions and keep aside.

Step 2

In cheesecloth, place the allspice, cloves and mustard seeds and tie together.

Step 3

In a pan, add the cheesecloth with remaining Ingredients and bring to a boil.

Step 4

Reduce the heat and simmer, uncovered for about 10 minutes.

Step 5

Place the mixture over vegetables and keep aside to steep for about 15 minutes.

Step 6

Transfer into a clean pint jar and keep aside to cool slightly.

Step 7

Cover and refrigerate.

SOUTH AMERICAN SALSA FROM SALVADOR

Prep Time: 5 mins- **Total Time:** 5 mins

SERVINGS: 6

NUTRITIONALS VALUE

Calories 15.2, Fat 0.1g, Cholesterol 0.0mg, Sodium 10.2mg, Carbohydrates 3.4g, Protein 0.5g

INGREDIENTS

- 1 C. radish, chopped in medium fine dice
- 2 tbsp fresh lemon juice
- 1 C. tomatoes, chopped in medium fine
- salt (to taste)
- dice
- 1/2 C. cilantro, coarsely chopped
- 1/2 C. red onion, finely chopped

DIRECTIONS

Step 1

In a bowl, mix together all the Ingredients.

Step 2

Serve immediately.

PINE NUT PESTO

Prep Time: 10 mins- **Total Time:** 15 mins

SERVINGS: 6

NUTRITIONALS VALUE

Calories 74.8, Fat 7.1g, Cholesterol 2.2mg, Sodium 38.6mg, Carbohydrates 1.8g, Protein 1.4g

INGREDIENTS

- 2 -3 C. radish tops, roughly chopped (
- 3 tbsp parmesan cheese, grated
- leaves)
- 2 tbsp pine nuts
- 2 -3 garlic cloves, quartered
- salt
- 2 tbsp olive oil
- pepper
- 2 tbsp lemon juice
- 1 tsp white sugar

DIRECTIONS

Step 1

In a food processor, add the radish leaves, garlic, olive oil and lemon juice and pulse till a thick paste forms.

Step 2

Add more olive oil if necessary to bring to your desired consistency.

Step 3

Add the sugar, cheese, nuts, salt and pepper and pulse till well combined.

Step 4

Refrigerate to blend the flavors.

CHICKEN WITH SEOUL(KOREAN CHICKEN)

Prep Time: 10 mins- **Total Time:** 40 mins

SERVINGS: 2

NUTRITIONALS VALUE

Calories 573.6, Fat 32.4g, Cholesterol 145.8mg, Sodium 2034.3mg, Carbohydrates 24.8g, Protein 40.4g

INGREDIENTS

- 1 medium daikon radish
- 2 tbsp sake
- 2 boneless chicken legs with thigh
- 1 tbsp sugar
- 1/2 tsp chili flakes
- 1/4 tsp mirin
- 1 tbsp vegetable oil
- pepper
- 1 crushed garlic clove
- 1 tsp sesame oil
- Glaze
- 2 C. chicken stock
- 3 tbsp soy sauce

DIRECTIONS

Step 1

Peel the daikon and cut into 1/2-inch half-moons.

Step 2

Cut the chicken into 1/2-1-inch pieces.

Step 3

In a large skillet, heat the vegetable oil over high heat and sauté the daikon and chicken.

Step 4

Stir in the crushed garlic and chili flakes.

Step 5

Reduce the heat to medium.

Step 6

Add the all the sauce Ingredients and cook, skimming off the fats from the top.

Step 7

When the sauce has nearly evaporated, drizzle with the sesame oil.

Step 8

Remove from the heat and serve.

ORANGE RADISH RELISH

Prep Time: 15 mins- **Total Time:** 1 hr 30 mins

SERVINGS: 6

NUTRITIONALS VALUE

Calories 57.4, Fat 4.7g, Cholesterol 0.0mg, Sodium 15.9mg, Carbohydrates 3.7g, Protein 0.4g

INGREDIENTS

- 2 C. radishes, thinly sliced
- salt and pepper
- 1/2 C. onion, chopped
- 3 tbsp orange juice
- 2 tbsp lime juice
- 2 tbsp fresh cilantro, chopped

- 2 tbsp canola oil

DIRECTIONS

Step 1

In a bowl, mix together all the Ingredients.

Step 2

Refrigerate, covered for at least 1 hour before serving.

SOUTH SALINAS SLAW

Prep Time: 10 mins- **Total Time:** 10 mins

SERVINGS: 10

NUTRITIONALS VALUE

Calories 41.1, Fat 1.5g, Cholesterol 0.0mg, Sodium 30.1mg, Carbohydrates 6.7g, Protein 0.7g

INGREDIENTS

- 4 C. shredded radishes
- 1 tbsp mustard oil
- 2 C. chopped yellow peppers
- salt and pepper
- 1 1/2 C. shredded carrots
- 1/2 C. white wine vinegar
- 4 tsp sugar
- 1 tbsp chopped fresh dill

DIRECTIONS

Step 1

In a large bowl, mix together the radishes, peppers and carrots.

Step 2

In another bowl, add the remaining Ingredients and beat till well combined.

Step 3

Place the dressing over the slaw and toss to coat well.

Step 4

Serve immediately.

KOREAN PICKLES

Prep Time: 15 mins- **Total Time:** 15 mins

SERVINGS: 1

NUTRITIONALS VALUE

Calories 95.8, Fat 0.3g, Cholesterol 0.0mg, Sodium 2373.7mg, Carbohydrates 23.1g, Protein 1.5g

INGREDIENTS

- 1 1/2 lbs daikon radishes, peeled
- 1 tbsp very thin matchsticks of peeled
- 1 bunch red radish, trimmed and each
- ginger
- cut lengthwise into 6 wedges
- 1 tbsp kosher salt
- 1/4 C. rice vinegar (not seasoned)
- 3 tbsp sugar

DIRECTIONS

Step 1

Cut the daikon in halves lengthwise, then cut crosswise into 1/4-inch-thick slices.

Step 2

In a large bowl, add the daikon, radishes and kosher salt and toss to coat.

Step 3

Keep aside at the room temperature for about 1 hour, stirring occasionally.

Step 4

Drain the radish mixture in a colander and return to bowl. (do not rinse)

Step 5

In the bowl of radish mixture, add the vinegar, sugar and ginger and mix till the sugar dissolves completely.

Step 6

Transfer the mixture into an airtight container and refrigerate, covered for at least 12 hours, shaking once or twice.

Step 7

This pickle can be preserved in refrigerator for up to 3 weeks.

MILKY RADISHES

Prep Time: 30 mins- **Total Time:** 45 mins

SERVINGS: 4

NUTRITIONALS VALUE

Calories 111.1, Fat 8.0g, Cholesterol 23.8mg, Sodium 87.8mg, Carbohydrates 7.3g, Protein 2.7g

INGREDIENTS

- 1 1/2 C. large strong radishes
- 2 tbsp butter
- 2 tbsp flour

- salt and pepper
- 1 C. milk

DIRECTIONS

Step 1

Wash the radishes, then trim and slice them.

Step 2

In a pan of boiling water, add the radishes and boil till tender.

Step 3

Drain well.

Step 4

In another pan, melt the butter.

Step 5

Add the flour, beating continuously.

Step 6

Stir in the milk, salt and pepper and bring to a boil, stirring continuously.

Step 7

Remove from the heat and stir in the radishes before serving.

FRESH VEGGIE PLATTER

Prep Time: 15 mins- **Total Time:** 15 mins

SERVINGS: 1

NUTRITIONALS VALUE

Calories 700.6, Fat 55.2g, Cholesterol 146.7mg, Sodium 1210.1mg, Carbohydrates 11.0g, Protein 41.3g

INGREDIENTS

- 8 oz. soft goat cheese
- 1/4 C. fresh Italian parsley, chopped
- 2 tbsp milk
- 1/8 tsp salt
- 1/2 C. radish, chopped
- 1/2 C. green onion, chopped

DIRECTIONS

Step 1

In bowl, add the cheese and milk and mix till creamy.

Step 2

Stir in the radishes, onions, parsley and salt.

ALABAMA SLAW

Prep Time: 20 mins- **Total Time:** 22 mins

SERVINGS: 4

NUTRITIONALS VALUE

Calories 104.3, Fat 7.5g, Cholesterol 0.0mg, Sodium 304.2mg, Carbohydrates 7.9g, Protein 1.9g

INGREDIENTS

- 8 oz. snow peas, cleaned, trimmed and
- 1/2 tsp Dijon mustard
- thinly sliced lengthwise
- 1/2 tsp sugar
- 1 red onion, thinly sliced

- 2 tbsp vegetable oil
- 1 bunch radish, cleaned, trimmed and
- 1/2 tsp sesame oil
- thinly sliced
- 1/2 tsp salt
- 4 tsp rice vinegar

DIRECTIONS

Step 1

In a large bowl, mix together the vegetables.

Step 2

In another bowl, add the remaining Ingredients and beat till well combined.

Step 3

Place the dressing over vegetables and toss to coat well.

Step 4

Serve immediately.

CANADIAN STYLE BROWN SUGAR CARROTS

Prep Time: 10 mins- **Total Time:** 30 mins

SERVINGS: 4

NUTRITIONALS VALUE

Calories 117 kcal, Fat 6 g, Carbohydrates 16.1g, Protein 1 g, Cholesterol 15 mg, Sodium 401 mg

INGREDIENTS

- 3 cups peeled and sliced carrots
- 1/2 teaspoon salt
- 2 tablespoons butter
- 1/2 teaspoon black pepper
- 2 tablespoons brown sugar
- 1 1/2 tablespoons chopped fresh dill

DIRECTIONS

Step 1

Get a frying pan and put your carrots in it. Then cover them in water and get everything boiling.

Step 2

Once the mix is boiling let everything cook until all the water is gone.

Step 3

At this point the carrots should be soft then combine in the pepper, butter, salt, dill, and brown sugar.

Step 4

Stir the mix so all the carrots are evenly coated.

Step 5

Enjoy.

A STEW IN DUBLIN

Prep Time: 30 mins- **Total Time:** 50 mins

SERVINGS: 6

NUTRITIONALS VALUE

Calories 161 kcal, Fat 3.1 g, Carbohydrates 31.3g, Protein 3.8 g, Cholesterol < 1 mg, Sodium < 1196 mg

INGREDIENTS

- 4 large carrots, thinly sliced
- 1/4 teaspoon dried thyme
- 2 large potatoes, thinly sliced
- 1/4 teaspoon dried basil
- 1 large onion, thinly sliced
- 1 teaspoon dried parsley
- 1/4 medium head green cabbage, thinly
- 1 teaspoon salt
- sliced
- ground black pepper to taste
- 2 cloves garlic, smashed
- 6 cups chicken stock
- 1 tablespoon olive oil

DIRECTIONS

Step 1

Get the following boiling in a larger pot like a Dutch oven: pepper, carrots, salt, potatoes, parsley, onion, basil, cabbage, thyme, garlic, olive oil, and chicken stock.

Step 2

Once the mix is boiling set the heat to low and let everything gently cook for 22 mins. With an immersion blender puree everything to form a soup.

Step 3

If you do not have an immersion blender you can puree the solids in batches with a conventional blender placing the puree into a 2nd pot until everything has been processed and combining the puree with the original liquid.

Step 4

Enjoy.

HONEY BUTTER BAE CARROTS

Prep Time: 5 mins- **Total Time:** 25 mins

SERVINGS: 4

NUTRITIONALS VALUE

Calories 402 kcal, Fat 23.3 g, Carbohydrates 50.7g, Protein 1.4 g, Cholesterol 61 mg, Sodium 249 mg

INGREDIENTS

- 1 (16 ounce) package baby carrots
- 1/2 cup brown sugar
- 1/2 cup butter
- 3 tablespoons honey

DIRECTIONS

Step 1

Get your carrots boiling in a saucepan covered with salted water. Let the carrots cook for 17 mins. After the time has elapsed empty the water and let the carrots sit in the pot covered for about 4 mins with no heat.

Step 2

Set the heat to low now and add in the butter. Let the butter melt then combine in the brown sugar and the honey. Continue to stir and heat the mix for 4 more mins.

Step 3

Enjoy.

NORTH AFRICAN CARROT SESAME APRICOT SPREAD

Prep Time: 10 mins- **Total Time:** 22 mins

SERVINGS: 10

NUTRITIONALS VALUE

Calories 65 kcal, Fat 2.1 g, Carbohydrates 12.1g, Protein 0.6 g, Cholesterol 0 mg, Sodium 210 mg

INGREDIENTS

- 1 pound carrots, peeled and thinly sliced
- 2 tablespoons fresh lemon juice
- 3 cloves garlic, thinly sliced
- 4 teaspoons toasted sesame oil
- 1 (2 inch) piece fresh ginger root, peeled
- 1 1/2 teaspoons ground coriander
- and thinly sliced
- 1/8 teaspoon cayenne pepper
- 3/4 teaspoon salt, divided
- 1/3 cup apricot preserves

DIRECTIONS

Step 1

Pour 2 cups of water in a larger pot then combine in you're: 1/4 tsp salt, carrots, ginger, and garlic. Get everything boiling then once it is set the heat to low, place a lid on the pot, and let the mix cook for 11 mins.

Step 2

Remove the liquids then add the mix to a blender. Also add in the cayenne, 1/2 tsp salt, coriander, apricot, sesame oil, and lemon juice.

Step 3

Puree the mix into a dip.

Step 4

Enjoy.

4-INGREDIENT CARROTS

Prep Time: 10 mins- **Total Time:** 1 hr

SERVINGS: 4

NUTRITIONALS VALUE

Calories 98 kcal, Fat 5.1 g, Carbohydrates 11.2g, Protein 3 g, Cholesterol 4 mg, Sodium 381 mg

INGREDIENTS

- 1 pound carrots, peeled
- 1/4 cup grated Parmesan cheese, or
- 1 tablespoon olive oil
- more to taste
- 1/2 teaspoon garlic salt

DIRECTIONS

Step 1

Cover a casserole dish with foil then set your oven to 375 degrees before doing anything else.

Step 2

Get a bowl, combine: garlic salt and olive oil. Combine in your carrots and toss them evenly in the mix. Layer your carrots into the casserole dish and cook them in the oven for 40 mins. Top the carrots with the parmesan evenly and continue to cook everything for about 7 more mins.

Step 3

Add some parmesan before serving.

Step 4

Enjoy.

ANIMAL CROSSING CARROT CANS

Prep Time: 20 mins- **Total Time:** 5 hrs 20 mins

SERVINGS: 4

NUTRITIONALS VALUE

Calories 74 kcal, Fat 0.1 g, Carbohydrates < 18.3g, Protein 0.9 g, Cholesterol 0 mg, Sodium 28 mg

INGREDIENTS

- 1/2 cup distilled white vinegar
- 2 tablespoons chopped fresh cilantro
- 1/4 cup white sugar
- 1 Thai chili pepper, seeded and chopped
- 1 small carrot, peeled and cut into
- matchsticks
- 1 daikon radish, peeled and cut into
- matchsticks

DIRECTIONS

Step 1

Get your sugar and vinegar heating in a pot until the sugar is evenly combined.

Step 2

Shut the heat and place the liquid in the fridge until it is cold.

Step 3

Get a jar and put your carrot and radish in the jar. Also place in the jar your chili pepper and cilantro. Add the vinegar into the jar and place the lid on them tightly.

Step 4

Place everything in the fridge overnight.

Step 5

Enjoy.

HONG KONG CARROT VEGETARIAN DUMP DINNER

Prep Time: 10 mins- **Total Time:** 8 hrs 40 mins

SERVINGS: 6

NUTRITIONALS VALUE

Calories 140 kcal, Fat 2.7 g, Carbohydrates 27.5g, Protein 3.3 g, Cholesterol 0 mg, Sodium 770 mg

INGREDIENTS

- 2 pounds baby carrots
- 1 teaspoon grated orange zest
- 1/2 cup orange juice concentrate
- 1 tablespoon Asian (toasted) sesame oil
- 1/4 cup tamari sauce
- 1 tablespoon honey
- 2 cloves garlic, minced

- 1 teaspoon minced fresh ginger

DIRECTIONS

Step 1

Simply all the ingredients to the crock pot of slow cooker and stir. Place the lid on the cooker and let the mix cook for 8 hours on low high then for 40 mins with High heat.

Step 2

Enjoy.

GARDEN PARTY SALAD

Prep Time: 15 mins- **Total Time:** 15 mins

SERVINGS: 4

NUTRITIONALS VALUE

Calories 47.7, Fat 1.8g, Cholesterol 5.0mg, Sodium 50.1mg, Carbohydrates 6.6g, Protein 2.5g

INGREDIENTS

- Salad
- 1/4 C. light sour cream
- 3 C. dark leaf lettuce
- 1 tbsp white vinegar
- 1 cucumber, sliced
- 2 tbsp chopped chives
- 3 C. fresh spinach
- fresh ground black pepper, as garnish
- 12 red radishes, sliced
- Dressing

DIRECTIONS

Step 1

In 4 serving plates, divide the lettuce and spinach.

Step 2

Arrange the cucumber slices and radishes over the greens.

Step 3

In a bowl, mix together the sour cream, vinegar and chives.

Step 4

Place the cream mixture over salad in each plate.

Step 5

Serve immediately with a sprinkling of the fresh black pepper.

RISING SUN CAKES

Prep Time: 1 hr- **Total Time:** 3 hrs

SERVINGS: 18

NUTRITIONALS VALUE

Calories 58.7, Fat 0.5g, Cholesterol 0.8mg, Sodium 297.1mg, Carbohydrates 11.8g, Protein 1.5g

INGREDIENTS

- 1/2 C. dried shrimp
- 1/2 lb rice flour
- 5 dried shiitake mushrooms
- 2 tsp salt
- 2 C. boiling water
- 2 C. chicken stock

- 3 lbs Chinese radishes

DIRECTIONS

Step 1

In a large heat proof bowl, add the boiling water and soak the shrimp and mushrooms. Peel and grate the radish directly into the chicken stock and simmer for about 15 minutes. Drain the chicken stock from the radishes, reserving into a bowl. Drain the soaking water from the shrimp and mushrooms, reserving into the bowl with stock.

Step 2

Mince the shrimp and mushrooms. In a large bowl, add the rice flour.

Step 3

Slowly, add the reserved liquids, stirring continuously till a slight thick mixture forms. Season with the salt and a little pepper.

Step 4

Stir in the radishes, shrimp and mushrooms.

Step 5

In a large pan, place the radish mixture and cook, stirring continuously till the mixture begins to thicken.

Step 6

Set your oven to 300 degrees F.

Step 7

Place the mixture into a 10-inch greased square cake pan evenly.

Step 8

With a piece of foil, cover the pan tightly.

Step 9

Arrange the cake pan in a water bath.

Step 10

Cook in the oven for about 1 1/2-2 hours.

Step 11

Remove from the oven and keep on wire rack to cool completely.

Step 12

Cut the cake into 1/2-inch slices.

Step 13

Heat a lightly, greased pan and fry the cake slices till browned nicely from both sides.

RADISH REJUVENATION

Prep Time: 15 mins- **Total Time:** 15 mins

SERVINGS: 5

NUTRITIONALS VALUE

Calories 82.3, Fat 4.2g, Cholesterol 5.3mg, Sodium 297.1mg, Carbohydrates 11.8g, Protein 1.5g

INGREDIENTS

- 1/4 C. light mayonnaise
- 3/4 C. sliced radish
- 1/4 C. nonfat sour cream
- 1/8 C. green onion, sliced
- 1 tbsp honey
- 1/4 C. toasted broken pecans
- 1/2 tbsp Dijon mustard
- 3 C. cabbage, finely shredded
- 2 C. romaine lettuce, finely shredded

DIRECTIONS

Step 1

For the dressing in a bowl, add the mayonnaise, sour cream, honey and mustard and mix till well combined.

Step 2

Refrigerate, covered to chill.

Step 3

For the salad in a large bowl, mix together the cabbage, romaine lettuce, radishes and green onions.

Step 4

Place the dressing over salad and gently, toss to coat.

Step 5

Serve with a sprinkling of the pecans.

MARIA'S MEXICAN TACOS

Prep Time: 10 mins- **Total Time:** 30 mins

SERVINGS: 4

NUTRITIONALS VALUE

Calories 521.9, Fat 21.5g, Cholesterol 33.3mg, Sodium 1043.0mg, Carbohydrates 69.6g, Protein 18.9g

INGREDIENTS

- 3 tbsp olive oil, divided
- 4 green onions, thinly sliced
- 2 garlic cloves, minced
- 1 serrano pepper, minced
- 1 (15 oz.) cans black beans, undrained

- 2 limes, juice of
- 1 (8 oz.) cans corn, drained
- 12 corn tortillas
- 4 tbsp cilantro, chopped
- 1 C. feta cheese, crumbled
- 1 tsp salt, divided
- 1/2 tsp pepper, divided
- 12 -15 radishes, halved lengthwise &
- thinly sliced

DIRECTIONS

Step 1

In a medium pan, heat 2 tbsp of the olive oil and sauté the garlic for about 1-2 minutes.

Step 2

Add the black beans with the can liquid, corn, 1 tbsp of the cilantro, 1/2 tsp of the salt and 1/4 tsp of the pepper and bring to a boil.

Step 3

Simmer for about 15 minutes.

Step 4

Meanwhile for the salsa in bowl, mix together 1 tbsp of the olive oil, 3 tbsp of the cilantro, 1/2 tsp of the salt, 1/4 tsp of the pepper, radishes, green onions, Serrano pepper and lime juice.

Step 5

Place the tortilla onto serving plates.

Step 6

Place the beans & corn in the middle of a tortilla and top with the salsa and feta evenly.

Step 7

Sprinkle with additional cilantro if you like.

FILIPINO STYLE TILAPIA

Prep Time: 5 mins- **Total Time:** 15 mins

SERVINGS: 10

NUTRITIONALS VALUE

Calories 112 kcal, Carbohydrates 13.4 g, Cholesterol 21 mg, Fat 1 g, Protein 13.1 g, Sodium 63 mg

INGREDIENTS

- 1/2 pound tilapia fillets, cut into chunks
- 3 cups water
- 1 small head bok choy, chopped
- 2 dried red chili peppers
- 2 medium tomatoes, cut into chunks
- 1 cup thinly sliced daikon radish
- 1/4 cup tamarind paste

DIRECTIONS

Step 1

Combine tilapia, radish, tomatoes, mixture of tamarind paste and water, chili peppers and bok choy.

Step 2

Bring the mixture to boil and cook for 5 minutes to get fish tender.

Step 3

Serve in appropriate bowls.

RADISHES, CUCUMBER & CABBAGE SPRING ROLLS

Prep Time: 20 mins- **Total Time:** 50 mins

SERVINGS: 12

NUTRITIONALS VALUE

Calories 9.9, Cholesterol 0.0mg, Sodium 48.9mg, Carbohydrates 1.7g, Protein 0.5g

INGREDIENTS

- 1/2 C. shredded daikon radishes
- 1 tbsp reduced sodium soy sauce
- 2 green onions, sliced thin
- 6 rice paper sheets
- 2 tbsps rice vinegar
- 1 1/2 C. bean sprouts
- 1 tsp Splenda sugar substitute
- cilantro
- 1 small fresh jalapenos, chopped
- shredded carrot
- 1/2 tsp toasted sesame oil
- 1/2 C. shredded carrot
- 1/2 C. short thin strips cucumber
- 2 tbsps snipped fresh cilantro

DIRECTIONS

Step 1

In a large bowl, mix together the green onions, radishes, jalapeno, rice vinegar, sesame oil and Splenda.

Step 2

In another bowl, mix together the cucumber, carrot, cilantro and soy sauce. Cover both bowls and refrigerate for about 2-24 hours, stirring once and drain them completely.

Step 3

Soak the rice papers, one by one in a bowl of warm water till soft and transfer onto paper towels. Place the rice papers onto a smooth surface.

Step 4

In the center of each rice paper, place the bean sprouts, followed by the radishes mixture and cucumber mixture evenly.

Step 5

Fold the inner sides of rice papers around the filling and roll tightly. Arrange the rolls onto a baking dish and cover with a damp towel.

Step 6

Refrigerate for about 2 hours before serving.

Step 7

Cut each roll in half and serve with a garnishing of carrot and cilantro.

BRITISH VEGGIE PASTRIES

Prep Time: 30 mins- **Total Time:** 1 hr 30 mins

SERVINGS: 4

NUTRITIONALS VALUE

Calories 687 kcal, Fat 44.7 g, Carbohydrates 55.4g, Protein 17.4 g, Cholesterol 155 mg, Sodium 859 mg

INGREDIENTS

- 1 recipe whole wheat pastry for a
- 1 tsp yeast extract spread
- double crust
- 1/4 C. milk
- 1/4 C. butter
- 1 egg
- 1 onion, thinly sliced
- 1/4 lb. shredded Cheddar cheese
- 1 carrot, sliced thin
- salt and pepper to taste
- 1 turnip, peeled and diced
- 1 egg, beaten
- 1 large potato, peeled and diced
- 1/4 lb. mushrooms, chopped
- 2 tbsp water

DIRECTIONS

Step 1

Set your oven to 400 degrees F before doing anything else.

Step 2

Divide the pastry dough into 4 equal sized portions.

Step 3

Place each dough portion onto a floured surface and roll in a square shape.

Step 4

In a large skillet, melt the butter on medium heat and sauté the onion for about 5 minutes.

Step 5

Stir in the carrot, turnip, potato, mushrooms and water.

Step 6

Reduce the heat and cook, covered for about 10 minutes, stirring occasionally.

Step 7

In a small bowl, dissolve the yeast extract in milk.

Step 8

Add 1 egg and beat till well combined. Add the yeast mixture into the cooked vegetables and stir to combine well. Cook, stirring continuously till the mixture becomes thick.

Step 9

Stir in the cheese, salt and pepper and remove from the heat.

Step 10

Keep aside to cool completely.

Step 11

Place 1/4 of filling over half of each pastry square.

Step 12

Fold the pastry diagonally and seal edges to secure the filling.

Step 13

Arrange the pasties onto a baking sheet and coat the tops with the beaten egg.

Step 14

Cook in the oven for about 30 minutes.

NORTH CAROLINA DINNER

Prep Time: 20 mins- **Total Time:** 9 hrs 10 mins

SERVINGS: 4

NUTRITIONALS VALUE

Calories 233 kcal, Fat 8.6 g, Carbohydrates 30.9g, Protein 11.2 g, Cholesterol 0 mg, Sodium 142 mg

INGREDIENTS

- 1 C. dried black-eyed peas
- 2 tomatoes, chopped
- 4 C. water
- 1 tbsp balsamic vinaigrette salad dressing
- 1 tbsp soy margarine
- 1 tbsp olive oil (optional)
- 1 turnip, peeled and chopped
- 1 bunch collard greens, chopped
- 2 cloves garlic, minced

DIRECTIONS

Step 1

In a large bowl of water, soak the black-eyed peas for about 8 hours to overnight.

Step 2

Drain well and rinse under cold running water.

Step 3

In a large pan, add the black-eyed peas, and enough with fresh water to cover on high heat and bring to a boil.

Step 4

Reduce the heat to medium-low and simmer, covered for about 40-60 minutes.

Step 5

Drain well.

Step 6

In a skillet, melt the soy margarine on medium heat and cook the turnip and collard greens for about 2 minutes.

Step 7

Add the black-eyed peas, garlic and tomatoes and cook for about 5 minutes, stirring occasionally.

Step 8

Serve with a drizzling of the balsamic vinaigrette and olive oil.

SKINNY VEGETABLES ROAST

Prep Time: 30 mins- **Total Time:** 1 hr 15 mins

SERVINGS: 10

NUTRITIONALS VALUE

Calories 210 kcal, Fat 6 g, Carbohydrates 38.9g, Protein 3.5 g, Cholesterol 0 mg, Sodium 121 mg

INGREDIENTS

- 1 butternut squash - peeled, seeded
- 3 parsnips, peeled and cubed
- and cut into 1-inch dice
- 3 turnips, peeled and cut into 1-inch dice
- 3 carrots, cut into 1 inch pieces
- 1/4 C. extra virgin olive oil

- 1 large sweet potato, cut into 1-inch
- kosher salt and pepper to taste
- cubes
- 1 rutabaga, peeled and cut into 1-inch
- pieces

DIRECTIONS

Step 1

Set your oven to 450 degrees F before doing anything else.

Step 2

In a large bowl, add the butternut squash, carrots, sweet potato, rutabaga, parsnips, turnips, olive oil, kosher salt and pepper and toss to coat.

Step 3

In a deep roasting pan, place the vegetable mixture.

Step 4

Cook in the oven for about 45 minutes, stirring once in the middle way.

www.ingramcontent.com/pod-product-compliance
Lightning Source LLC
LaVergne TN
LVHW060823170826
845678LV00010B/1883
9798436622217